Perfect

This book is dedicated to Kat and Tom with love.

Perfect

Feeling Judged on Social Media

ROSALIND GILL

polity

First published in 2023 by Polity Press

Polity Press
65 Bridge Street
Cambridge CB2 1UR, UK

Polity Press
111 River Street
Hoboken, NJ 07030, USA

ISBN-13: 978-1-5095-4970-2
ISBN-13: 978-1-5095-4971-9 (pb)

A catalogue record for this book is available from the British Library.

Library of Congress Control Number: x

Typeset in 11 on 14pt Warnock Pro
by Cheshire Typesetting Ltd, Cuddington, Cheshire
Printed and bound in the UK by 4edge Limited

For further information on Polity, visit our website:
politybooks.com

Contents

Acknowledgements

First and foremost, I would like to thank all the young people who generously gave up time to take part in this research. I absolutely loved talking with you! It was a pleasure and a privilege to hear about your experiences and to be entrusted with your stories. I have tried to treat your words with tenderness, care and respect, while also changing names and some details to protect your confidentiality.

The university where I work, City, University of London, gave me access to some funding to carry out this research, which was crucial in being able to offer a (very) small token of thanks to participants, and also to pay for transcription. I would like to express my personal appreciation to Miguel Mera and Cassie Sipos for this support.

I am also extremely grateful to Whitney Francois-Cull who worked with me on designing the survey that was carried out in May–June 2020, much of which was done under very tough lockdown conditions. Together we have co-authored a book chapter entitled 'Media do not represent me' that is published in another volume. It was great working with you, Whitney, and I look forward to collaborating on more research and writing in the future.

Polity was brilliant – as always – and I would like to express my sincere gratitude to Mary Savigar and Stephanie Homer for their care and attention every step of the way. Thank you also to the two anonymous reviewers who gave me feedback on the first draft of this book and to Ian Tuttle for his careful copyediting.

As I was writing *Perfect: Feeling Judged on Social Media*, I was lucky enough to have some invitations to present the work-in-progress in different places – many of them via video platforms – and I would like to thank the organizers of, and participants in, talks in Vienna, Rome, Essex and Sardinia for discussing the ideas with me. These spaces and conversations have become even more vital during the last few years. My special appreciation to Emma Gomez Nicolau for inviting me to UJI in Castellon, Spain, for a brilliant event on young people's resistance. It has been a pleasure getting to know you, Emma, and your close colleagues, especially Maria-Jose Gamez Fuente and Sonia Nunez Puente. An invitation to Athens in September 2022 was equally inspiring and another example of those precious moments when academic connections become friendships. Thank you to Liza Tsaliki and Despina Chronaki, and also to Sean Redmond. A big shout out also to the amazing women that make up the collective organizing 'Algorithms for Her': Sophie Bishop, Zoe Glatt, Zeena Feldman, Ysabel Gerrard, Kate Miltner and Rachel Wood – a vital space of intersectional critique, and the first place I will talk about my work *after* this manuscript is (finally) submitted!

The pandemic prevented travel further afield, and I have sorely missed colleagues and friends in Australia and New Zealand – especially Lisa Adkins, Ginny Braun, Julia Coffey, Bridget Conor, Amy Dobson, Ngaire Donaghue, Sue Jackson, Akane Kanai, George Morgan and Sarah Riley. I'm very grateful for our collaborations and connections, and I would like to express my especial thanks to Akane and Julia for reading a draft of this book, and for being such a pleasure to work with, think with and be with. Sue: I know you don't need an acknowledgement to feel my love and care, but here it is anyway.

Other close friends and colleagues also generously read and commented on drafts. Warm, appreciative thanks to Sara de Benedictis, Hannah Curran-Troop, Rachel O'Neill, Annelot Prins and Christina Scharff for taking the time to engage so thoughtfully and for sharing your insights.

Thank you also to my friends Andy, Chris, Elizabeth, Juliet, Veronica, Beverley, Lesley, Najiba, Roisin, Louise, Ann and Hazel. Thank you to darling Sylvia who was with me at the start of this research but not at the end. Thank you to my Jude, with appreciation and sadness.

This book was written at a moment of multiple converging crises that made life very hard for many people. For me personally it has been a time of loss and grief. In this context, more than ever, friendships have been vital and precious, and, in addition to the friends mentioned already, I would like to say a huge thank you to four women who are not just brilliant scholars who each generously read a draft of this book, but are also the most extraordinary friends, without whose love, support and sense of humour this time would have been even tougher. Thank you Catherine, Jo, Sarah and my beloved Shani for everything.

Finally, my love and gratitude beyond words to Kat and Tom to whom this book is dedicated.

Preface

I just wanted to say that I feel very seen and recognized by this research. You have captured my life on social media exactly. I really wish my parents and teachers could have heard about research like this – then they would know what it's like.

Oh. My. God. How did you know?! It's like you've been living with me and my friends and you've somehow got access to all our deepest feelings about how it is. That is my life!

This is a book about young people's lives on social media. It is a book about connection and community, but also about loneliness and exclusion. It is about the pleasure and affirmation of nice comments and shares, but also the worry and anxiety about 'getting it wrong'. It is about wanting others to 'like' your photos, but feeling it is impossible to live up to current appearance standards. It is about care and friendship, but it is also about competition, harassment and microaggressions. It is about feeling you have to be perfect, but also having to be real. It is about wanting to share how you are feeling, but knowing you have to post only your 'best life' or your 'highlights reel'. It is about longing to belong and be part of 'what is happening' but feeling watched and judged for absolutely everything.

These are some of the paradoxical and ambivalent feelings that I heard about between 2020 and 2022 during an intense period[1] of listening to young people from all over the UK, via a combination of open surveys and in-depth interviews. More than 220 people aged between 18 and 28 took part in the research. I heard mainly from young women – and they are the primary focus of this book – but also from some young men, and from people who identified beyond or outside the gender binary. I heard from people of diverse heritages and backgrounds, whose parents or grandparents were born not only in the UK but also in Africa, the Caribbean, Bangladesh, India or Pakistan, in Ireland, Greece or in Eastern Europe, and in China, Iran and the Middle East. I heard from folk who identified as heterosexual, as bisexual, as lesbian, gay or pansexual; from people with disabilities and those living with mental or physical health challenges; from people with different religious backgrounds or no religious affiliation at all; from some whose families were comfortably off, to many people who were struggling to make ends meet. I spoke with a nail technician and a construction worker, a fashion assistant and a research scientist, a fitness instructor and a media worker, a primary school teacher and an animal welfare officer. I interviewed young people setting up their own micro-businesses, and those who worked in bars, shops or restaurants – and those who also did all or some of these jobs while also being students.

The young people who took part in this research were articulate, thoughtful and insightful. They spoke fluently and with passion about their lives on social media, about lives lived, increasingly, they said, 'on my phone'. Their social media might not be the only thing going on at any one time, but there were alerts and notifications pinging in constantly while they worked, studied, watched TV, cooked or spent time with family or friends. Their favourite platforms were the first things they looked at each morning and the last thing they checked before they went to sleep, and many, many times in between. The vast majority got their news from social media, ran their social lives via the platforms, and pursued interests, work lives and activism on their socials too, as well as what most described as many hours each day of 'random browsing'. This book is about their lives.

Understanding social media lives

It is a strange fact that while social media are rarely out of the headlines, and are also heavily researched by academics, marketers and others, it is nevertheless hard to find books that really capture the *everyday experiences* of young people as they manage social media lives. When I was finishing this book in late 2022, news about social media was everywhere: Elon Musk had just taken over Twitter, Meta had sacked 12,000 staff, and the Online Safety Bill was making its way through the UK Parliament. At the same time, TikTok was expanding rapidly in the social media sphere, with petitions circulating demanding that Instagram 'stop trying to be TikTok', and journalists were discussing the new popularity of BeReal. Yet amidst all the reporting and commentary it was still rare to get a glimpse of ordinary, quotidian, mundane experiences on social media.[2] I wondered at first if I had just missed the books that did this, if I was somehow looking in the wrong places. In all honesty, I also experienced my own kind of 'feeling judged' moment, wondering if the reason I hadn't come across a book like this one was because it was too trivial, too obvious or not important enough to write. But when I presented this research at different conferences and events, young people – including students of media – reassured me on both counts. They told me that I hadn't missed the literature that engages with their experiences – or at least they hadn't found it either. And they described the jolts of recognition they experienced hearing me talk about this research. 'That's me', they told me, 'That's my life you are describing.' I have included some examples of these kinds of comments at the start of this chapter; they not only offered the comfort that I was onto something worth writing about, but also, more importantly, an affirmation that I had listened, heard and represented young people's experiences in a way that was meaningful to them.

Parents also wanted to talk with me after such presentations. 'You have articulated exactly what my 20-year-old is going through', said one senior academic after hearing me give a lecture about this research at a conference. During a coffee break she read out to me a WhatsApp message her daughter had sent her the previous evening. The message described feeling that she was never going to be pretty enough, popular enough or successful enough in her relationships, and said how alone with it all she felt, how everyone else seemed to be doing so much better. She sounded just like many of the young women I interviewed for this book, and her mother did not know how to help her. As media scholar Amy Shields Dobson has argued, parents are often anxious about their children's social media lives, but their anxieties do not necessarily align with the scripts they have been given for what they 'should' feel anxious about: sexting, stalking, stranger danger. Instead, they worry about the 'intensities and pressures of constant contact with peers in the digital era',[3] often feeling helpless to know how to offer support, especially as they have not themselves grown up at a time when so much of life was mediated through platforms like Instagram, Snapchat or TikTok.

Polarized research

Looking to the research may not offer much help with these quotidian experiences, with the everyday 'texture' of social media life. A lot of research about young people and social media polarizes around two contrasting accounts, linked to different academic disciplines. Research in Psychology centres on investigating the risks, dangers and harms of social media for young people, particularly young women.[4] Frequently these studies get news coverage, with rarely a week going by without media reports of the negative effects that Instagram or TikTok are having on girls' and young women's mental health and wellbeing, and highlighting rapidly increasing rates of eating disorders, anxiety and depression.[5] Against this, Media and Cultural Studies experts typically face down this sense of alarm. They warn against the tendency to create 'moral panics' about social media – reminding us that a similar sense of crisis has been associated with every new medium from film to video games to the internet. They caution against treating young people as passive cultural dupes who mindlessly imitate what they see online. In contrast to psychologists, such researchers tend to reassure the public and policy-makers that 'the kids are alright': they are savvy and sophisticated and highly media literate.[6]

To the new student or anyone else trying to find out 'what the research tells us' about young people's experiences on social media, it is perplexing to encounter these opposed positions. Their different takes relate not only to academic discipline, but to the methods adopted and even the language used. For example, psychologists often use loaded terms like 'exposure' to refer to being on social media, which implicitly sets it up as something bad. Reading such research, I often feel uncomfortable about the way it sometimes blames or even criminalizes young people, with talk of their 'risky behaviours', and with the frequent references to social media 'addiction', a concept which not only robs agency from young people but also works to pathologize them. Conversely, some Media and Cultural Studies scholars may take an emphasis upon agentic 'active audiences' so far that it is as if these giant corporate platforms simply offer a smorgasbord of options from which young people freely pick and choose, or against which they are 'resistive, tactical or refusing digital media users'.[7] In the understandable efforts of some media and communication experts to refute popular conceptions of the 'homogeneity', 'unthinkingness' or 'gullibility'[8] of audiences – a project which I wholeheartedly support – it sometimes feels as if a sense of struggle and vulnerability is lost. Yet what young people told me was that they are critical and highly social media literate, but they *also* feel caught or trapped in a set of relations not of their choosing.[9]

Perfect: Feeling Judged on Social Media

Perfect: Feeling Judged on Social Media intervenes to restore a sense of ambivalence and struggle to understandings of social media lives, and also to highlight the conditions of (im)possibility in which young people operate. It looks not at social media themselves but at young people's experiences on their socials, using an approach that foregrounds their own words and stories. The book builds from Media and Cultural Studies traditions, including a commitment to respect, and to valuing how young people 'make their ways' through the complicated terrains they encounter both on- and offline. But it is rooted in a commitment to careful listening to young people's own accounts, experiences and feelings in all their complexity, including the ethical responsibility to attend to expressions of pain and distress which form part of the picture of how young people experience their lives on and off social media. In this sense the book is also informed by psychosocial studies and especially by an interest in affect, emotions and feelings.[10] This, then, is not an either/or but a *both/and* contribution – one that is attentive to power and to difference, to pleasure and despair, to connection and loneliness, and everything in between. It builds on my own research over three decades, and also on a growing body of feminist scholarship that is critical, intersectional, theoretically and methodologically creative, attentive to the complexities and intensities of feelings and lived experiences, and to understanding digital culture and everyday life.[11]

The young people whose words are quoted in this book were generous in what they shared with me. They talked about their diverse and evolving social media, the influencers they follow, what they watch on Netflix and YouTube, their passionate engagement with #BlackLivesMatter, their love of cooking videos, their anger at the media, the photos they take and how they edit and filter them before posting. They reflected on Instagram versus Reality trends, body positivity, their mental and physical health, on comparing themselves with others, and the 'codes of honour' of the night out photo. They discussed the pandemic, the lockdowns and isolation, and they also talked about the media they used to help get them through – from Zoom quizzes, to TikTok challenges, *Drag Race* and the latest series of *Married at First Sight Australia* (which was screening in the UK when I was carrying out the first half of the interviews).

As they talked about their lives, I was repeatedly impressed by how skilfully they navigated multiple demands, platforms and relationships. They were expert and adept, the archetypal 'digital natives' – to use the cliched phrase. Yet despite this sophistication, their experiences were far from straightforward, but instead were full of ambivalence, contradictions and struggle. Some of this originated in the material conditions of their lives – frightening amounts of student debt, precarious housing, worries about getting or keeping jobs – all of which had been exacerbated by the pandemic, and by the cost-of-living crisis. Yet there was also a huge array of dilemmas that related to other issues – to questions of how to 'be' in the world, how to relate to others, how to present themselves. These are not the trivial issues they are sometimes assumed to be – particularly when women are the subject – as if they are a matter of mere vanity or narcissism. Rather they go to the heart of what it means to be human – and they consumed much of young people's energy and attention as they deliberated about their social media lives and how they manage them.

Perfect: Feeling Judged on Social Media is about their experiences, illustrated throughout with young people's own words and stories. In making sense of these, I discuss their friendships and the contradictory dynamics of care, competition and sometimes cruelty that characterize them. I examine how young women in particular feel caught in webs of mutual surveillance, checking each other out and policing each other in subtle ways, and how they also feel watched by men, by advertisers and by the social media platforms themselves.

I also document the sheer energy, work and attention they put into running and managing their 'always on' social media lives alongside working, studying, relationships, etc. – and particularly the labour that goes into maintaining profiles on multiple platforms.

This book puts the notion of the perfect centre stage because it was something that absolutely everyone talked about and with great passion. Instagram-perfect-beauty made young women feel alternately angry, despairing, ashamed, and like they will never be good enough. The relentless circulation of picture-perfect photographs of women's bodies indicates something of the power of the image at a moment in which unprecedented numbers of new images are created every day. This power is reinforced by a beauty industry that has moved from cosmetics counters and beauty clinics to the intimate space of the phone, promoting the requirement to look your best at all times – whether through editing and filtering apps like Facetune that will digitally enhance your photos, or via surgical procedures or 'tweakments' like fillers, Botox or cosmetic dentistry that young women told me are 'pushed' to them endlessly.

But the perfect is not only about physical appearance. Rather, as cultural theorist Angela McRobbie has argued, it operates as a 'horizon of expectation' for all women, and it operates across all aspects of life and experience.[12] This book shows how imperatives to post a perfect life included every aspect of you: the right food, the right drinks, the right locations and venues, the right friends, and even the right attitudes and dispositions – with the mandate not just to be visible, but to present as happy, fun and sociable, no matter how you actually feel. These unwritten rules and expectations about perfection produced intense anxiety among many young women I interviewed, as they experienced the quite reasonable worry that they would in some way 'get it wrong'. Young women told me that besides being watched all the time, they also felt constantly 'judged' and lived in fear of making a mistake that might be called out by others. These experiences exacerbate the broader struggles with mental health that many participants – like others of their generation – were experiencing.

It is often said by developmental psychologists that adolescence and youth should be periods for experimentation and for trying new ways of living and being. In critical cultural theory, too, there has been an emphasis on the productive possibilities of 'failure' to resist or subvert power structures or suffocating norms – for example, Judith Jack Halberstam's *Queer Art of Failure*[13] seeks to interrogate and dismantle the elevation of 'success' in neoliberal capitalism. What this book shows, however, is that young people, particularly young women, are operating in a context in which there is a prohibition on failing, and instead they are being called upon to live up to ever more restrictive norms of behaviour and self-presentation. The flipside of the emphasis on perfection, then, is the terror of 'falling down', the FGW (the 'fear of getting it wrong'). There is no roadmap or guidebook to help young people navigate this fraught and contradictory territory. Little wonder, then, that so many young women described feeling so alone and so silenced. I hope this book will contribute to challenging that.

Introduction

Perfect: Feeling judged on social media

I don't want to see these perfect people. It just makes me feel rubbish. And I know if I see too many images, it makes me question myself... Yes it just feels like this image I've been fed into my head of what it is to be perfect. It's probably the single biggest thing that makes me miserable. (Elizabeth, 23)

Introduction

Elizabeth was 23 at the time I interviewed her. She had just finished Medical School, and, like many other health professionals, had been asked to start work immediately, even before graduating, because of the crisis wrought by the pandemic. On the sunny afternoon when we spoke, she was preparing to start work as a junior doctor in the Accident and Emergency department of a large hospital in the north of England. Despite her understandable trepidation, she seemed happy, relaxed and pleased to be doing something that she hoped would 'make a difference'. Our conversation ranged over many topics besides her imminent new job: she spoke of her love of cycling, her passion for cooking, her involvement in climate change activism – and of course her social media. Her socials had helped her during the pandemic, she said:

> It is actually just so weird when I think of it, but it does make me feel better and it makes me feel nice at this time, during this lockdown period where I haven't really seen my friends, just to be like, oh, people are still seeing me, like I've got a nice photo or whatever . . . I do find myself just looking and looking at it [social media].

Just a few minutes later, however, this positive evaluation seemed to have evaporated. Elizabeth had a catch in her voice as she told me how painful and difficult she finds things on social media – above all, the beauty standards, the conformity to stereotypes and the pressure to post a perfect life:

> It has made me miserable for so long, and it makes me feel really angry because I haven't chosen these stereotypes. I feel like they've been fed to me. And I think it's, yes, because you're just presented all the time with pretty much a replica of what it looks like to be perfect, and then variations of that perfect.

It made her feel 'rubbish', she said. She felt 'upset' and 'like other people are going to judge me'. Elizabeth was choking back tears as she explained how trapped she feels, and also how complicit she believes she is in perpetuating images and values she herself rejects. 'I haven't chosen this', she kept telling me, 'but I feel like the damage is already done . . . it gets inside you . . . and . . . the worst thing is . . . I know that I judge other people too.'

Elizabeth's experience is far from unique. This short extract from our interview vividly expresses many of the themes this book addresses: the profound ambivalence about social media that many young women described as a 'love-hate relationship'; the painful tyranny of perfect images and how low and depressed they can make you feel; the pervasive anxiety about being judged by others, particularly friends and peers; the anger and eloquent criticism that many expressed about the beauty industry, and about the erasure and exclusion to which they are subject; and, despite this articulate analysis and critique, the sense of being caught or trapped in social media lives they have not chosen. In this introductory chapter, I set out briefly the themes and arguments of the book, already touched upon in the preface. Next, I discuss the particularities of the context in which I conducted this research. I then set out the principles on which this research is based which foreground listening to young people, valuing diversity, thinking intersectionally and writing accessibly. Finally, I outline the structure of the book.

Themes and arguments

Picture perfect: the power of images

Compared with previous generations, today's young women live in a world where visual images of women's bodies are ubiquitous in media, public space and especially online. With 3.2 billion photographs posted every single day, *the power of images* was something young women talked about a lot. The phrase *'it's all too perfect'* is one I heard repeatedly from participants in this research. Media of all kinds, but particularly social media platforms, were seen as trafficking in images of perfection that are 'unrealistic' and 'unattainable', and that contribute to a pervasive sense of never being good enough. 'I don't look like that, I'll never look like that', 27-year-old Letitia told me, capturing a widely held view. 'I see all these perfect bodies in bikinis and it makes me feel really low'. Others said they feel 'ashamed', 'overwhelmed' and 'like a failure'.

Young women are eloquent in their *critiques of 'perfect' images*, and their rage is palpable. As one woman wrote in the survey: 'we are constantly being told we are not thin enough, not pretty enough, too many spots, not enough boob, not enough bum, too bigger thighs ... it goes on and on'.[1] They are *skilful* at deconstructing photographs, whether that is to question the authenticity of the picture (e.g. filtered, edited, botoxed) or to challenge the norms it represents (e.g. whiteness, slimness, upper-class aesthetics). But, as Elizabeth explained, they still feel 'trapped' by the pressure somehow to live up to these images: that is, their anger at the injustice of this pressure does not nullify its impact; that is, they are *struggling*, they are *critical but caught*. Instead, in their posts, they strive to present their own version of the perfect, which many described (deceptively simply) as a 'nice photo' – one that is characterized by a beautiful yet natural and apparently effortless appearance, with pictures that should look 'amazing' but spontaneous, and not appear to have been (unduly) filtered or edited.

Posting your best (perfect) life

An ideal post is not only picture perfect, but should also display coolness, fun and popularity. It must be carefully curated but not look as if it is the result of any particular care or design. It means being in the right locations with the right people, with good-looking 'instagrammable' food and drinks, and an always 'positive' disposition – no matter how they actually feel. The perfect, then, is not only about appearance but also about displaying the 'right' kinds of feelings and attitudes, through pictures but also through humorous, self-deprecating and relatable[2] captions and stories. Time and again young women told me that they struggle with what they experience as the *impossible demands* to be 'perfect' and yet also to be 'real'.

Being watched

Paralleling the pressures to post images of a perfect life was the experience of *being watched*, which I heard about again and again from young women. They felt watched and evaluated in public space, both on- and offline, as well as in venues such as bars and clubs. This could occasionally be a pleasurable experience, but for many young women it was unpleasant and stressful – they talked about being 'stared at' and described feelings that ranged from embarrassment to fear. For those whose social media settings were public, this also meant regularly being subject to unwanted attention, lascivious or nasty comments, and unsolicited 'dickpics'. Indeed, the routineness of this *harassment* – and the extent to which it was dismissed as 'just creeps', 'weirdos' or 'some random guy' – was shocking to me as a researcher, precisely because so many women took it to be such a mundane feature of their lives that it apparently hardly merited discussion.[3] Being trolled and publicly put down or shamed was, by contrast, experienced as deeply distressing.

Feeling judged

A different form of being watched was that experienced among friends and peers. Young women repeatedly expressed the sense of being under surveillance in a way that was both evaluative and forensic. Most young people expected their photos to be subject to a critical scrutiny that could border on hostility. In fact, one of the experiences discussed most frequently in the interviews was that of *feeling judged* by others – perhaps especially by friends who might reasonably be expected to have warm and affectionate feelings towards them. They told me how easily comments could be misinterpreted on their socials, and *friendships go awry*. Being 'talked about' negatively was obviously an upsetting experience, and young women discussed the particular dynamics of this, which could involve an Instagram image being screenshotted and then viciously dissected in a private WhatsApp or Snapchat group. As 21-year-old, white, animal welfare officer India put it 'Honestly, it's awful. Every single thing anyone does is judged . . . Even if you're just being yourself – and people are all for being yourself – they're still going to judge you anyway.'

New ways of seeing

This sometimes hostile but always forensic scrutiny of others is facilitated by the affordances of smartphones – particularly their magnification features – as well as the platforms them-selves which can 'reveal' if photos have been filtered. More generally, these critical forms of looking have been inculcated and tutored by a rapidly expanding beauty industry, which has trained young women to 'see', that is to practise forms of look-ing, that are quite new and historically unprecedented in their attention to micro-surveillance of the face and body. *Perfect: Feeling Judged on Social Media* builds on my previous research on beauty apps to argue that young women practise new ways of seeing that are markedly different from any that have gone before. Many were painfully aware of having been schooled by makeup videos, transformation challenges and adverts for myriad cosmetic procedures from tooth whitening to lip fillers – as well as by the aesthetics of the platforms themselves – in precisely the forms of critical and evaluative looking that they themselves experienced as painful and judgemental. This is an 'upgraded' form of what Susan Bordo called a 'pedagogy of defect'[4] – namely the way that women are repeatedly taught to see themselves through a lens that centres what is wrong – wrinkles, blemishes, large pores, cellulite, untidy eyebrows, etc.

This forensic gaze is also applied to their own appearance. Young women had a hypercritical approach to how they looked, and they told me that they actively sought to identify 'flaws' and 'fails' in photos they considered posting. Their worry that they might miss something meant that they checked in with others first – usually one or two close friends – who could be trusted to tell the truth, e.g. 'I've seen you look better babe' – which 23-year-old Bipasha told me was 'friend code' for 'do not under any circumstances post this picture!' This is one of the *practices of care* among friends that young women discussed most often. It stood out from other mentions of friends' and peers' *competitiveness or even cruelty* – once again highlighting the fraught, contradictory set of relations young women described navigating.

The work of being social

This book also draws attention to the intense work involved in this endeavour – how much thought, time and energy goes into preparing and posting images. This might involve careful planning of outfits and locations and timings, multiple attempts to get the right picture (selecting from tens or even hundreds of takes), considerable care in editing a photo using in-app tech or other editing software such as Facetune or VSCO, designing a caption, timing the post appropriately, and then checking back regularly to gauge reaction. An important body of research explores these practices in relation to social media influencers, examining the various forms of work that are required: emotional or affective labour, aesthetic labour, relational labour, authenticity work and intimacy labour. However, little current writing has devoted similar attention to the work of being social as it is practised by 'ordinary' social media users. *Perfect: Feeling Judged on Social Media* argues that there are significant continuities with influencers in the work expected of young women in a ubiquitous, always-on social media environment.

Fear of getting it wrong (FGW)

The fear of posting a 'bad photo' that is not attractive enough or good enough pulsed through young women's talk. The *fear of getting it wrong* reflects the *conditions of (im)possibility* in which young people live. There were so many ways of getting it wrong and 'failing' in front of their friends and peers, such as seeming to be trying too hard, posting too much or not enough, appearing vain, being 'fake', posting something that does not get enough likes, or showing distress and thus being deemed 'attention-seeking'. A sense of coruscating anxiety animated many young women's accounts of posting to their socials. Even after checking with friends, posting was still an intensely anxious endeavour. Once an image was posted, many described how fear and doubt would eat away at them, how they would either become paralysed by anxiety and not look at their phone, or, conversely, would refresh the app repeatedly every few seconds to 'make sure it was ok' and to see if it was getting likes and comments. They offered embodied and visceral accounts of this experience – particularly at night – with stories of hearts pounding, adrenaline pumping and the restless anxiety that made falling asleep impossible after having posted something.

Structures of feeling (bad)

The emotionally charged nature of these experiences was striking. The interviews were punctuated non-verbally with gasps and sharp intakes of breath, with hands flying up to cover faces, with occasional sobs and small strangulated sounds of distress, amidst other presentations of self that were utterly poised, and moments that were full of laughter. The levels of anxiety young people experienced were at times devastating. Several participants told me about their own particular mental health challenges, together creating such a long list that it reads like the index of a psychiatry textbook: attention-deficit hyperactivity disorder (ADHD), obsessive-compulsive disorder (OCD), generalized anxiety disorder (GAD), autism spectrum disorders (ASD), eating disorders, depression, social anxiety disorder (SAD). This reflects the current situation in which more young people than ever before have mental health diagnoses, while at the same time there is an unprecedented crisis in mental health services.[5] Although many participants talked about the more open public discourse on mental health, several also felt that theirs struggles were largely taboo and they still could not talk openly about particular challenges without risking negative consequences such as being accused of seeking attention.

Another dominant feeling was the sense of being *caught or trapped* in sets of social relations in which one did not wish to participate – already seen in Elizabeth's words at the start of this chapter. I also remarked to several friends while doing the interviews that I was struck by how many times young women used the words 'exhausting' and 'draining' to describe their experiences of what were supposed to be enjoyable and sociable experiences. Lily, 20, for example, described a cycle where she tried to participate actively in a network of friends by posting on Instagram, but found it 'draining'. She explained:

I mean I'll try to take pictures, but I don't, I just don't like them. Like I'll try to take two or three, and I'm like, no, I don't like . . . and I'll just give up on it. It's just because the more you get into it, the more pictures you don't like of yourself. No that's a bad angle. No that wasn't a good picture. And it just puts you down even more. So I just try to avoid taking as many pictures.

This sense of *fatigue and being drained* was not unusual. Pushing us beyond an emphasis on individual pathology to a more social or cultural reading, several participants who were not otherwise depressed told me that their socials often made them 'spiral down'; they also expressed a sense of pointlessness or *futility*. This prompted me to ask many of my interviewees whether they had considered just not bothering – perhaps just quitting social media. A typical older adult's question! However, this course of action was troubling to most. It was not *entirely* unthinkable, and, as I describe later in the book, there was a sense of struggle and flux and change which could involve *temporarily* deleting the apps or turning off comments or notifications. But for many, walking away would have meant cutting off and isolation – a kind of social death, even – which participants understandably wanted to avoid. Therefore, the refusals and deletions tended to be short term: not 'quitting' but 'temporarily deleting', 'stepping back' or 'taking a break' or undertaking a 'cleanse'. These strategies or 'small acts of engagement'[6] (or indeed disengagement!) go to the heart of debates about young people and social media to which this book contributes.

The context

The research for this book was begun at an extraordinary time at the height of the Covid-19 pandemic. When the research began in May 2020, the global pandemic had already killed hundreds of thousands of people worldwide, and more than 40,000 in the UK. Countries across the world were living under 'shelter in place' orders, with lockdowns and states of emergency across multiple nations. At the time this research was launched in the UK, residents had been ordered to 'stay at home, save lives and protect the NHS'. Schools and nurseries were shut; universities had moved all activities online; bars, restaurants, cinemas, theatres and leisure facilities were all closed; and all but essential stores were shuttered, with public transport running a skeleton service for 'keyworkers' only. The vast majority of people in the UK had been in 'lockdown' for

8 weeks already, allowed out only once a day for exercise and to buy essential supplies. By the finish of the project, when this book was submitted, more than 212,000 lives had been lost to Covid in the UK,[7] and two million people were continuing to suffer symptoms of long Covid.[8]

Against this historically unprecedented background, the research set out to explore young people's use of media, social media and smartphones, with a particular focus on questions about bodily practices, appearance and mental health and wellbeing. The design of the research included both a survey, designed to generate a breadth of responses, and interviews to offer deeper insights. The research would have been important at any time, but the unique context of the Covid-19 pandemic and lockdown gave it a particular urgency. Day after day, reports were published highlighting the devastating mental health impacts of the pandemic on young people: their education suddenly halted, their freedoms curtailed, with many experiencing financial hardship, emotional difficulties, bereavement.

In a pandemic whose impacts were shaped by egregious inequalities that cross-cut age, class, race, gender and disability, young people faced many of the same challenges as other groups in relation to the pandemic, but they suffered disproportionately from some: they were significantly more likely to be in insecure and rented housing than older groups, they were more likely to be in precarious forms of employment, and they were highly likely to have experienced disruption to their education. Intersectional inequalities relating to race, class and gender produced higher rates of infection and mortality among BAME (Black, Asian and minority ethnic) groups and working-class populations, while women bore the brunt of job losses, and increased caring responsibilities, as well as the horrifying rise in violence against women. Elements of these wider trends were seen vividly in this research: one Black participant, furloughed from her job in retail, became the main carer for a grandparent who was 'shielding'. Another two young white women had to move back in with family after losing their jobs.

In some ways, young people's facility and familiarity with online tools and platforms might be said to have better pre-pared them (relative to older groups) for the lockdown period in which so many aspects of life moved online – including much work, education, psychological and health services, and social lives. In other ways, they experienced heightened pressure and distress, including anxieties about the future, financial worries and unemployment. This was exacerbated across the duration of this research by a growing cost-of-living crisis marked by dramatic rises in food and energy costs and soaring inflation that reached more than 10 per cent as this book was being completed. As one *Guardian* writer observed, the label 'cost of living crisis' is 'too tame' and 'too polite' to capture the 'brutal' realities of 'losing homes and everything'.[9] Everyday journalistic accounts, including her own, document the spectre of soaring rents and mortgages, of people choos-ing between 'eating and heating', of food banks running out of food. They also catalogue the punitive impacts of multiple crises related to austerity, Brexit, pandemic, war and govern-ment policies, including devastating cuts to public services, with local councils on the verge of bankruptcy, shortages of food and medicines, basic infrastructure crumbling, and more than 7 million people waiting for urgent hospital care, at the time I write this.

None of the young people I interviewed was homeless or hungry – and in this sense they were more privileged than a completely representative sample. But plenty of them were struggling financially, taking extra work or side hustles, cutting back on going out – with all the attendant impacts on social isolation – and even adopting the well-documented strategy of going to bed early to save on heating costs. In this sense the research reveals something about 'the ordinary within the

extraordinary'[10] in a moment of multiple crises that are represented or mediated in real time.[11]

Besides the pandemic and associated restrictions, and a
growing cost-of-living crisis marked by rapidly increasing food
and energy costs, the research context was also dramatically
shaped by two events that formed the harrowing contexts
to this study: the murders of George Floyd in May 2020 and
Sarah Everard in March 2021. The killing of George Floyd by
police in Minneapolis on 25 May 2020 occurred just after this
research went live. Although the killing and injuring of African
Americans by police is horrifyingly anything but rare, it is
widely acknowledged that George Floyd's murder was a pivotal
moment in the US and worldwide.[12] The footage of his murder,
and of his repeated protestations 'I can't breathe', recorded on
phones and shared via social media, generated waves of outrage, and inspired a huge public mobilization and resurgence
of Black Lives Matter protests across the globe, including in
the UK. Some of the pain and rage about persistent racism
and structural injustice made its way vividly into responses to
survey questions: expressed as anger about the whiteness of the
media, the failure of conventional news organizations to report
fairly on the protests and on histories of racism, colonialism and
slavery, and about the cynicism of brands attempting to appropriate the cultural energy of the Black Lives Matter movement
through a kind of 'corporate wokewashing'.[13] The answers to
several free or open questions in the survey were a particular
locus for these discussions – in which many respondents wrote
eloquently and at length about these issues. Experiences of
racism in the UK context were also discussed in the interviews,
in a moment stained by the British government's notorious
'hostile environment'; the outrage of the Windrush scandal in
which people who had migrated to Britain from the Caribbean
in the 1950s–1970s were detained or deported after decades
living legally in the UK; and the growing litany of organizations
recognized as 'institutionally racist'.

The abduction, rape and murder of Sarah Everard, also by a serving policeman, forms another grim context for this research, that may be less well-known outside the UK. At 9.30 PM on 3 March 2021, Sarah Everard set out to walk home from a friend's house in South London. She never made it. After a week of searches and intense media interest, Sarah's remains were found in Kent, and a police officer was arrested and charged with her rape and murder. In the days following this, there was an outpouring of rage and grief from women across the UK, about Sarah's murder, the wider prevalence of violence against women, and the failure of successive governments to take it seriously as an issue. There were discussions in the national Parliament, and vigils and protests across the country, which, as in the Black Lives Matter protests the previous summer, took place during – and in spite of – strict lockdown and social distancing rules. In the aftermath of this murder, social media became key sites for sharing information, research and personal stories of women's experiences of harassment and abuse.[14] A widely shared statistic was the finding from a UN Women UK study that 97 per cent of women aged between 18 and 24 in the UK had been sexually harassed in a public place.[15] The site Everyone's Invited garnered more than 15,000 testimonies from young women about rape and sexual violence in a matter of days.

In interviews I carried out in March and April 2021, young women spoke passionately about the impact this murder had had on them, on what they saw and posted on the topic, and on how the discussions in the wake of Sarah Everard's murder resonated with their own personal experiences. Some participants also reflected critically and with anger about the disproportionate attention given to the murder of a white, middle-class, blonde-haired and conventionally attractive young woman, compared with comparable attacks on Black and working-class women, including 21-year-old Blessing Olusegun, whose death in 2021 received little coverage, and

Bibaa Henry and Nicole Smallman who were also murdered in a London park the previous year. Not only were police grievously slow to investigate the latter, but, horrifyingly, two officers at the scene photographed their mutilated bodies and shared the images via WhatsApp, with the caption 'dead birds'.[16] Using *pointedly understated* language betokening her controlled rage about this, Helena, a white queer-identified teacher who took part in this research, offered an intersectional reading of the double standards in media reporting, in which Everard became the archetypal 'missing white woman'[17]:

> Obviously it's a tragedy, there's nothing to be taken away from that. But I just think that people only really care now because she was a pretty blonde white woman, and actually young Black girls go missing all the time and no one cares. And not just young Black girls, young girls that aren't white, and boys actually that aren't white, no one cares, and that makes me a little sad as well. So I think I'm not taking away from the tragedy of her death, it's more that it highlights how other deaths aren't really a tragedy for many people, which I find sad.

Scholar and activist Moya Bailey has coined a powerful term that captures what Helena is talking about – 'misogynoir' – a word designed to highlight the 'particular venom' and 'denigration' directed at Black women in and beyond media because of their gender and race.[18,19]

Research principles

Three key principles underpin this research. These are: a focus on listening to young people; the importance of diversity; and an intersectional approach. Below I discuss each in turn, and also introduce – in broad terms – the research participants.

Listening to young people

If, for physicians, the primary principle that guides their work is to 'do no harm', then for researchers interested in people the equivalent priority must be to listen. As the novelist and art critic John Berger famously put it: 'listening is what's important. Listening to a story is primary, the listening is always primary'.[20] This is all the more urgent at a time when young people are so disparaged, with hostile and contemptuous terms such as 'snowflake' widely used,[21] and 'generation wars' are manufactured in which older people are invited to watch as 'millennials' and 'Gen Z' are pitched against each other.[22] Sociologist Les Back,[23] author of *The Art of Listening* (2007), has written of his engagement with young people: 'you listen to them, you care about them ... You give them time.' Such principles have also guided this research.[24]

Too often research is *about* young people without seeming to start from young people's *own* concerns. There are panics about ('too much') screen time, about (the 'narcissism' of) selfies, about (the 'dangers' of) sexting. By contrast, this research sought to understand how young people themselves think and feel about a range of issues, practices and experiences, in a manner that owes a debt to the disability movement's slogan 'nothing about us without us'. This commitment was built into the research via several strategies, most notably involving young people in the initial design of the research methods and allowing space for multiple open questions in the survey, which had a significant impact on the experiences young people shared.[25] Extraordinarily, more than 1,500 comments were left in response to open questions – some of them long and detailed – demonstrating the extent to which questions and topics seemed to have 'struck a chord'.[26] Young people were eager to share their experiences, and to communicate beyond the limitations of what can be conveyed via multiple choice questions and Likert scales.

In the interviews, participants also had the chance partially to shape the conversation. Beginning with a broad open question 'Can you tell me which social media you have', I sought to follow young people's interests and be open to the directions in which they took the discussion, while also covering a general list of topic areas on which I wanted their views. Furthermore, towards the end of each interview I explicitly asked each participant about topics that were important to them that they had not felt had been covered, and, more generally, if there was anything else they'd like to discuss. Many young people took this opportunity to talk about issues and concerns that were important to them. Memorably, one participant checked some notes they had made before the interview to ensure they had discussed all the issues they wanted to cover. Another said she would like to discuss an experience of having sexual images of her shared without her consent. A third said she would like to talk more about how she was affected by autism and by not being neurotypical.

Interviews are, like all of social life, striated by power relations. These relate to institutional features of the research relationship (e.g. who gets to select participants, ask questions, make analyses, etc.) as well as to key aspects of identity such as gender, race, disability and class. Such topics have been subject to extensive scrutiny and consideration by feminist scholars, who have drawn attention to the fact that research is ineluctably shaped by power, *and* have interrogated the apparent 'obviousness' of the way that these relations operate or come into force in any particular context.[27] This research is no exception, and my identity as a white, middle-aged, cisgender professor undoubtedly conferred privileges, as well as shaping the dynamics of interviews in particular socially and culturally inflected ways. At the same time – and in no way contradicting this – the interviews were also often very special, warm, intimate and intense interactions for participants as well as for me. Many remarked on how much they enjoyed the interview, how vital it had been as a space to think and reflect, and several commented with surprise on what had come up, saying that they had not realized how strongly they felt about something before our conversation. Many told me that they do not really have anyone to talk with about the difficulties they experience, particularly as being seen to struggle can be disparaged as 'attention-seeking'. More than one interviewee described the interview as 'like a detox' for them.

As I show in this book, many young people feel very alone in their social media lives; they feel reluctantly positioned in relations of competition and judgement with their peers, required to live up to impossible standards and, as such, it is easy to believe that everyone else has things sorted. In this context, my age and (thus) social distance – alongside particular personal characteristics (such as friendliness and empathy) – facilitated interviewees to talk in ways they described as being a result of feeling that it was a 'safe' and 'non-judgemental' space. Several implicitly (and sometimes explicitly) identified me as someone 'like my mum' and I was assumed to be both benign and a social media novice. This latter attribution was incredibly helpful, meaning that interviewees patiently described the difference between posts and stories on Instagram, or what comes up on TikTok's For You screen, or how they think its algorithm may be changing. These explanations were not only thoughtful and helpful, but were extremely illuminating contributions.

Valuing diversity

A second key principle that shaped the research is that of valuing diversity. It was imperative that this research should hear about the experiences of a wide range of young people from different ethnic and racial backgrounds, of different sexual orientations, disabilities, religious affiliations, geographical regions and social classes. Far too much research focuses predominantly on white, cisgender, heterosexual, middle-class and non-disabled people, and in research on body image and social media there has been a particular focus on white, middle-class girls. By contrast, this research *actively solicited* participation from under-represented groups through its recruitment strategies using personal networks and contacts, via social media or word of mouth, as well as a research recruitment platform. It has produced a research population that is notable for its diversity.

Full responses to the survey came from cisgender women – that is women's whose current gender identification aligns with the one they were assigned at birth (82 per cent) – and the survey also recruited men (16 per cent) and those who identified as nonbinary, gender-fluid or genderqueer (2 per cent). Women's lives are the primary focus of this book,[28] while other experiences are also discussed at points. Gender is cross-cut by multiple other axes of difference including age, race, sexuality and disability. Although the age range for participation was 18–30, this was strongly skewed to a younger age group, with 53 per cent of participants aged 18–21, and a further 40 per cent aged 22–27. Compared with official statistics from the 2021 census, people of colour and LGBQ+ folk were *over-represented* as proportions of the UK population compared with white and heterosexual-identified participants.[29] White participants comprised 72 per cent of survey respondents, with 27 per cent from BAME[30] or racially-minoritized backgrounds including African, African-Caribbean, Indian, Bangladeshi and Pakistani, Iranian, Arab and Chinese, as well as mixed heritages. Twenty-one per cent of participants in the survey identified as LGBQ+, with a variety of self-identifications including lesbian, gay, bisexual and pansexual. Six per cent of those who completed the survey identified as disabled.

In addition to the survey, I conducted thirty interviews with a diverse range of young people. The interviews were mostly carried out via a video platform, which, as well as being necessary at first because of the pandemic, also made it easier to talk with people from all over the UK – in three of the four nations (England, Wales and Northern Ireland) and multiple different regions. Almost half of interviewees belonged to BAME groups, and they were also diverse in relation to other identity characteristics. They ranged in age from 18 to 28, with most being in their early twenties (20–23). Just under half the participants were students, reflecting the broader situation for this age cohort, and others worked in fashion, retail, hospitality, medicine, construction, animal welfare, teaching, media, performing arts, and science, and/or were setting up their own businesses.

It is important to note that interviewees were also diverse in their orientations to social media, which ranged, at one end of the spectrum, from three individuals with minimal activity on a small number of platforms, to the other in which five were working as brand ambassadors, pursuing careers as influencers or otherwise dedicating immense time and energy to their socials. This range of differences in orientation to social media is discussed more fully in the next chapter.

Towards an intersectional analysis

The third key principle underpinning the research is a commitment to intersectional analysis, by which I mean a commitment to thinking about power and social relations as involving multiple axes (e.g. gender, race, sexuality, class, disability, age, geography, health status, nationality, etc.), which are not simply 'additive' but exercise their own distinctive force and effects on experience. As Avtar Brah and Ann Phoenix put it, the concept of intersectionality signifies 'the complex, irreducible, varied and variable effects which ensue when multiple axes of differentiation – economic, political, cultural, psychic, subjective and experiential – intersect in historically specific contexts. The concept emphasizes that different dimensions of social life cannot be separated out into discrete and pure strands'.[31] For analysts this means paying attention to differences and recognizing that these are organized hierarchically but also in what Patricia Hill Collins has called a 'matrix of domination'. It represents

> the critical insight that race, class, gender, sexuality, ethnicity, nation, ability and age operate not as unitary, mutually exclusive entities but as reciprocally constructed phenomena that in turn shape complex inequalities.[32]

In relation to gender, then, intersectional analysis involves the necessity to think sexism *with* racism, ageism, classism, homophobia, (dis)ablism. Not only is it politically vital, but it also should produce 'better' research because '[i]ntersectionality as an analytic tool gives people better access to the complexity of the world and of themselves'.[33]

Aspiring to an intersectional analysis and taking it seriously is a complex endeavour that requires attentiveness to multiple power relations. I am helped in this by the articulate and critical interventions of many of my participants who were themselves trying to think beyond unitary categories of identity. As I discuss in chapter 2, participants offered intersectional analyses of 'perfect' media images, commenting upon multiple elements of identity including race, skin colour, gender identity, disability, body size, class and visible markers of religion. Moreover, in discussing their own locations, several participants were keen to highlight not just their different positionalities, e.g. 'Black, Muslim and a Londoner' or 'working class, white and disabled', but also to reflect on the way that different features of their identity may confer disadvantage *and* privilege. For example, one woman discussed the discrimination to which she was subject as a lesbian, but also how she benefitted from her white, femme, conventionally attractive appearance. Another interviewee of British and Nigerian heritage described the particular discomfort (verging on shame) she experienced in some situations at feeling favoured over darker skinned women. There was, then, particularly, but not exclusively, among participants located outside the dominant or the normative (e.g. whiteness, middle-classness, heterosexuality), a significant attentiveness to issues of power and difference.

Overview of the book

This chapter has introduced the main themes and arguments of the book. The chapter has also set out the distinctive context for this research, briefly introduced the diverse participants who took part in the project and set out the principles that underpin my approach. *One final principle I have tried to adhere to is to write as clearly and accessibly as possible.*

Chapter 1 offers a sense of the range of orientations participants had to social media, highlighting the differences among them in which platforms they used, how long they spent on their socials, whose or what accounts they looked at or followed, how often they posted, and so on. The chapter shows the thoughtfulness and deliberation that characterizes participants' social media lives, on questions such as how to manage different aspects of the self on different platforms, whether to have public or private settings, and how they managed social media lives during the pandemic.

Chapter 2 continues the emphasis on young people as critical and media literate, but this time with a focus on their political (small p) engagements and the nuanced and intersectional manner in which they make sense of the (social) media landscape. Although the research did not set out to talk to 'activists', many of the participants demonstrated extraordinarily eloquent critiques of contemporary culture. The chapter shows that, alongside criticisms that 'it's all too perfect', there were also multiple analyses of the exclusions of social media, and of the experiences of invisibility or erasure these produced – relating to race, gender identity, disability and sexuality.

The third chapter zooms in on the beauty industry, looking at the very different ways in which it materializes in young women's lives – from the ubiquity of the photo-editing apps (such as Facetune), which nearly everyone used before posting a selfie, to the power of influencers, the interest in makeovers and the uptake of transformation 'challenges' – which proliferated at the height of the pandemic. The chapter shows, in young women's own words, the new force of a beauty industry that is no longer just 'out there' in cosmetics stores or beauty clinics but is 'right here on my phone', telling women that they are not pretty enough and that they need to work harder and buy more. The chapter looks at how the pandemic worked to loosen appearance imperatives, but also, paradoxically, became a time in which participants decided to invest in their looks via longer term strategies of self-optimization, e.g. straightening ones teeth via Invisalign. Finally, it also shows how smartphones are implicated in an intensification of a 'pedagogy of defect', and the emergence of new forensic ways of seeing.

Issues connected to looking and seeing are further explored in chapter 4, which focuses on young women's multiple experiences of being watched, evaluated and subjected to intimate intrusions, which one participant memorably called 'all the eyes and all the hands'. The chapter also considers the way that the hyper-critical surveillance of women's bodies across culture more generally operates to intimidate and discipline young women, underlining the sense that their appearance is the most important thing about them, and the feeling that they will never be good enough.

Chapter 5 looks in detail at young women's experiences of posting, exploring how they are shaped by the idea of the perfect. The chapter shows that posting practices are mediated by judgements that are simultaneously aesthetic (it has to look good), affective/emotional (it has to depict the right kinds of feelings or dispositions), and relational (shaped by friendships that entangle care and competitiveness). The chapter looks at the work that goes into creating a post – planning, taking pictures, editing and 'producing' them – drawing out the similarities between participants who were micro-influencers, and other young women who invested a similar amount of planning, time and care. The chapter concludes with a focus on the widely shared experience of 'feeling judged' for one's posts, drawing out the way that friends may be allies and supporters but are also perceived as hostile scrutineers ready to pounce on any 'fail'.

Chapter 6 is entitled 'Fear of getting it wrong', and, in a vivid indictment of the levels of anxiety among young women, it documents the myriad fears expressed in relation to posting on social media. Time and again young women told me how judged they feel on social media, and they itemized all the many ways they could fail – even when they thought they were posting a 'nice photo' or that it was 'a good post'.

Bringing together what participants said about the pressures to be perfect, the anxieties about posting, the sense of feeling watched and feeling judged, I hope this book goes some way to illustrating the intensely difficult social relations that young women are having to navigate – and are doing so well, but at considerable cost. In the concluding chapter I draw together the themes of the book, highlighting the pervasive anxiety and exhaustion that young women described. I discuss how their critiques were stymied by the isolation and loneliness they experienced amidst this sociality, and how caught and trapped they felt by its norms. I argue that the difficulty of translating their sophisticated critical orientations into more powerful forms of resistance results from the conditions of impossibility within which they operate, in which the feeling of being alone and the prohibition upon failure are devastating mechanisms of silencing. But I conclude hopefully with a discussion of young women's quiet refusals.

1

Life on my phone

*RG: So, is it all right if I just jump straight in with my first ques-
tion? Which is: which social media are you on?*

*Nadine: I think I'm on everything, every possible thing. So,
Instagram, Twitter, Snapchat, TikTok, Facebook. Does
YouTube count? I have a YouTube account. Just everything.*

The oldest participant in this research was born in 1991; the
youngest in 2002. Dubbed 'Generation Z', these 18–28-year-
olds have grown up with social media; their experiences of life
are intimately entangled with particular platforms, and shaped
by different 'platformed socialities'.[1] MySpace launched in
2003, Facebook in 2004, YouTube in 2005, Twitter in 2006,
Instagram in 2010, Snapchat in 2011, and TikTok in 2017 –
to name only the most popular socials. The definitions and
boundaries of what counts as social media are contested and
dynamic,[2] from early analyses of 'social networking sites'[3] to
contemporary understandings of a 'social media paradigm'.[4]
As Zoetanya Sujon argues in her excellent introduction to
social media, it is important to challenge the 'obviousness' of
what should be included under the heading.[5] Here I use my
participants' own definitions of what counts. LinkedIn, Reddit,

Pinterest, Tumblr and Vine were mentioned by some participants, as well as newer platforms including Houseparty, which
launched in 2020 and came into its own during the Covid pandemic, BeReal, which launched in 2020 and became popular
in 2022, and even Zoom, which had become host to university
lectures, pub quizzes and reunions during lockdowns.

Young people narrated their lives in relation to the meaning that social media platforms had for them, laughing about
former selves so eager to get a Facebook account that they
had lied about their age, and telling self-deprecating stories of
their first Instagram, dominated by 'cringeworthy posts' about
now-embarrassing pop star crushes. Others spoke with pride
about how long they had been able to maintain a 'Snapchat
streak' with a friend – in one case (Anna, 21) 6 years. Nowadays
Facebook seemed staid and boring, most told me, and they
were only on it to stay connected to family or to access organizations (such as university societies and clubs) that required
it. Most experienced their current lives as mediated ever more
intensely by Instagram, Snapchat and TikTok, closely mirror-
ing data on social media use from Statista and other bodies.[6]
Almost 90 per cent of the young women in this study had
at least one Instagram account, the large majority also used
Snapchat, and there was barely an interviewee who did not
comment on TikTok's 'addictive' properties. The research
coincided with the rapidly rising popularity of the platform
and its move away from being seen as dominated by tween or
teen dance crazes.

In this chapter I aim to give a sense of the broad contours of
young people's social media lives. In the first half of the chapter,
I discuss the platforms they use, when and how they use them,
who they follow. There was immense variation among young
people's social media practices, from some who barely engaged,
to others who were on their socials 'every hour of every day'.
While some participants used only one or two platforms, many
others, like Nadine above, who was unemployed after recently

graduating, told me they were on 'everything'. There were also huge differences in how people felt about their socials, with some expressing 'love', others 'hate' and most 'ambivalence': 'it's a tug of war for me', said Lynne, while Letitia said it was 'a love–hate relationship'.

Faced with this kind of variation and diversity, many researchers turn to typologies of social media use. Categorizing social media use is big business, worth millions to those who want to address, sell or market to this youthful demographic. Academics and marketers have generated hundreds of typologies to attempt to capture and represent the diverse ways in which people use and engage with social media platforms, looking at features such as when they started using social media, how much they use different platforms, whether they seek out information or entertainment, whether they contribute or just 'lurk' – and myriad other dimensions. Classifications proliferate, describing 'innovators' and 'early adopters', 'minglers' versus 'devotees', 'alpha socializers' and 'attention-seekers', as researchers seek to create persuasive knowledge that can be sold to platforms and brands as representing the truth of the complex and varied ways people engage with their socials.

Perfect: Feeling Judged on Social Media troubles this perspective. It notes how problematic such categorizations are, how they work by squeezing people into boxes, and repressing the extent of complexity, contradiction and ambivalence. For example, as I will show, some of the most avidly enthusiastic of Instagrammers – as measured by their time spent, the number of posts, the number of followers and the degree of engagement – may also, simultaneously, express distress, frustration and loneliness in relation to their social media. One of the micro-influencers interviewed for this research described feeling that it had become a 'chore' having to post so often, and another feared that she was getting to a point where 'you have Instagram *instead of* a life' (Nadine, 23). Rather than pigeonholing people into social media 'types', this research focuses on the *range and distribution of practices and feelings* to better illuminate how young people are experiencing 'life on my phone'.

The second half of the chapter will also demonstrate the thoughtful and sophisticated way that individuals engaged – their attention to different platform affordances and different audiences and levels of intimacy, their deliberations about temporality and privacy settings, the careful manner in which they managed social media lives.

The diversity of social media practices

In the Introduction, I briefly described the diversity of my sample in relation to identity characteristics including race and ethnicity, gender identity, disability, class, religion, mental health and sexual orientation. The sample was also diverse in terms of my participants' relationship to social media of various kinds. Five of my thirty interviewees characterized themselves as 'micro-influencers'[7] with between 12,000 and 85,000 followers on Instagram and/or TikTok, and were earning money from brands and/or receiving clothes, shoes and other products in return for posts, Stories, Reels or TikToks. Each had negotiated and signed contracts with one or more brands, from a global sportswear company, to several major British fast-fashion brands, to 'modest' fashion companies selling clothes to style-conscious young Muslim women. These participants were active across social media and posted several times a week. At the other end of the spectrum, three of my interviewees, aged between 21 and 23, used only YouTube, Snapchat and Facebook and posted rarely on the latter. One of these was India, 21, a trainee animal welfare officer. She told me:

> India: Well, I'm one of the people who doesn't have every-
> thing. I don't have all social media. I don't really want to get

involved with everything. I have Facebook and Snapchat and that's pretty much it for social media things. I don't really use Snapchat at all ever, but I do use Facebook every day. Yes. That's it really. I don't have Instagram or Twitter or anything like that.

RG: Interesting. Can you tell me a bit about why that is? Was there a deliberate decision?

India: Yes, definitely, because with Facebook I feel like that's enough for me. I spend stupid amounts of time scrolling through it sometimes, but I just find that every time I'm on Facebook, I feel like I've wasted time just looking through things and I get quite depressed . . . I don't want to feel more like that if I have all social media.

In general, the platforms that participants used most were Instagram, Snapchat, TikTok, as well as Facebook, especially Messenger. Young people also spent a lot of time on YouTube watching videos. A significant proportion also used Twitter, and several people mentioned spending time looking at Pinterest, Tumblr and BuzzFeed. Ruby, a white 27-year-old scientist, who also had a parallel life as an acrobatic performer, said:

God, *all* of them. I have Facebook, Twitter, Instagram, I'm on LinkedIn. I don't have Snapchat, that's the one that I don't . . . I don't know, I'll have a look and see what I've got. Facebook, yes. I've got Tumblr. Tumblr, Twitter, Facebook, Instagram are the main . . . Oh, and LinkedIn are the mains ones that I use.

Bipasha, 23, who was of South Asian heritage, worked in the social media department of a large company and her job involved her posting content every few minutes across various platforms. But for her personally, when she was not at work, it was all about Instagram:

Definitely Instagram 90 per cent of the time. I use it for *every-thing*, for news, for entertainment, for fashion, for shopping, literally everything. Instagram is my main source.

Sitting on my phone

Many people said they were on their phone 'all the time'. They described waking up with it in the morning, and going to sleep with it at night and having it on them or with them at every moment. Nazanin, 18, a British student of Iranian heritage, said 'my phone is always next to me'. She said she found it 'draining', but also 'hard to put down'. Bianca, 18, a Black Londoner, told me:

I'm on it every hour of the day but for short or longer periods. So, there will be times where I'm on it for five minutes, there's nothing on there. There're times when I'm on it for two hours, three hours. So, it depends. But if I'm at college I would say I don't use it as much, or work, I don't use it during those times. But when I'm at home, it's constantly, oh, let me go watch this video or let me go and text my friends, go on FaceTime.

A few participants described how their families tried to set limits on their phone use, which they – in general – appreciated. Joanne, 23, a white painter and decorator, who had moved back home early on in the pandemic after losing her previous job, said her Welsh family were 'very traditional' and that there were 'strictly no devices at the table'. She described how this rule came about because of her dad's focus on 'good manners', and said that she had come to really value the time away from her phone. She explained she enjoyed 'family meals', asking and being asked 'how was your day?' Several other people also expressed deep ambivalence about the isolated sociality of social media, and the amount of time they spent on their own, in their room, on their phone. One participant, who was a fashion influencer whose contracts with brands meant she had to post different outfit pictures four or five times every week, told me nevertheless that she sometimes wondered why she spent so long alone on her phone, and wished she was downstairs with her mum and their two dogs. Trying to articulate what made her at times 'depressed' with her social media, Holly, another micro-influencer, said:

> I don't know what it is. I don't think it's what I'm reading. It's not what I'm seeing. It's just the fact that I'm not living in the moment. I'm not interacting with my family or I'm not outside getting fresh air. I'm just sitting on my phone like this. I don't know. It's not something that I'm seeing online or what I'm reading. It's just the fact that I'm not elsewhere actually doing things.

Almost everyone said they were on their phones much more during the pandemic, with estimates given ranging from 3 hours to 14 hours a day, especially during lockdowns when they were not going out, when some had been furloughed or lost their jobs, and when universities were operating online only.

Random browsing

Participants' top uses of social media were to stay in touch with their friends, to follow celebrities and influencers, to keep up with news, to share resources about activist campaigns they supported and to undertake 'random browsing', which many said could devour hours at a time. TikTok's algorithm was mentioned repeatedly in this respect, with the sense that young women would decide 'Right, this is the last thing I'll look at' but then be offered more and more content that was difficult to ignore. Addiction metaphors were ubiquitous in my participants' discourse – but nearly always said with humour rather than real concern. While browsing, many people found it very hard to recall or account for what they looked at on social media. Helena, 28, was typical in this respect. She said she spent many hours each day on various platforms, but when I asked her about what she tends to look at, she struggled at first to answer:

> Oh, I don't know, I consume so much of it now, and now that I'm thinking about it I can't really think of where it generally starts. I would say it might start with an interview with a celebrity that I'm interested in watching. And then escalates to more of the things they've done, or more interviews with other similar celebrities, something like that. I watch comedy skits and clips that are funny, but again there's no real rhyme or reason to those.

This captures vividly the nature of random browsing which, on the one hand, could keep giving you more of the same, or, on the other, could take you somewhere completely unexpected. It also speaks to the experience of social media feeds as an ongoing flow. Naturally, what people engaged with varied enormously, with some people enthusing about baking, others about fashion and beauty content, some about music or gaming. The responses were also shaped by the particular context of the pandemic and lockdown, as well as by the resurgence of #BlackLivesMatter activism.

Influencers and activists

In the survey young people reported that the influencers they were most likely to follow were bloggers, celebrities, activists and reality TV stars from shows such as *Love Island*, *Drag Race* and *Made in Chelsea*. They explained the main reasons for their choices were to get inspiration (by far the largest set of responses), to be motivated (e.g. in fitness), for lifestyle tips (e.g. food, beauty or fashion) and to keep up with what is happening. Lynne, 19, a white university student told me about who she follows:

> I do follow quite a few influencers. Well, yes, and celebrities. But I'm trying to follow more activists now, so I think it's about equal activists and influencers. But because influencers post more content, I . . . see more of that. Like Molly-Mae from *Love Island*. Jourdan Dunn who is a model. Who else? I follow Kylie Jenner . . . because everyone follows Kylie Jenner . . . And then Gigi Hadid. And then I follow quite a few magazines. I follow ID magazine and Dazed magazine. Plastic magazine. Stuff like that.

The following of influencers was understood as a divisive issue. Indeed, Lisa, a 20-year-old art student, who had been referred as an interviewee by a friend of a friend, confessed that when she heard about this research, she didn't think she would have much to contribute:

> I wasn't sure how helpful I'd be, because I know a lot of my friends follow models and that kind of celebrity, but I don't really follow anyone like that. . . . I'm not generally that interested. It maybe sounds a bit snobbish because sometimes I see on my explore page, a Kardashian will come up or something. And sometimes I do get drawn in and I'm like, how can this person's life be real? But it's more in a this just seems insane kind of way, rather than . . . I know a lot of my friends follow people who've been on *Love Island* and stuff like that, and I guess they're more real.

Some other participants, like this London student, were also critical of celebrity culture and of influencers:

> In particular with influencers, like typical influencer type girls, it's typical pictures that are very forced posed photos where

they're head to toe in a specific outfit and a full face of make-up, hair done ... The influencer accounts that is *all* they post really.

And they post pictures holding their new handbag to pro-mote the sponsorship they have with the handbag and things like that and I don't, I'm not interested in that (Soraya, 20)

Others interviewees charted a very different path by follow-ing mainly body positive models, LGBTQ+ activists, antiracist activists. Letitia, 27, a Black woman who worked in retail, told me

So, I follow a huge array. So, I follow a lot of influencers, mainly body positive influencers. A lot of influencers who discuss things like skin care. For years, well, my whole life, whole teen-age life and adult life now, I've suffered from really bad acne. And for a long time, it really affected me, really, really did affect me. And, I suppose, one thing that has helped me is social media and normalizing it. It [acne] isn't just this horrible thing that people make it out to be. It [social media] has really helped me accept it and break the stigma.

In turn, Alex, a 20-year-old nonbinary participant explained how they use social media for information, support and inspi-ration particularly from other LGBTQ+ people:

I have Facebook and I use that, occasionally for posting things but not that often. I often scroll through it and see what other people have posted and I follow different accounts, some LGBT accounts. I'm in some trans-specific Facebook groups, where we talk about various stuff to do with socially transitioning or medically transitioning or whatever, acceptance from people and stuff like that. I usually use Facebook just for chatting to people on Facebook Messenger.

I follow friends, I follow some influencers that I like, I follow some body positivity Instagrams and some Black Lives Matter Instagrams. I follow a lot of other LGBT people who are posting that kind of content and different stuff like that. I don't use Snapchat. I tried it once and did not like it. I use YouTube, just to watch YouTubers that I like. Usually either funny content or LGBT-specific content.

A strong social justice orientation characterized many participants' perspectives. It was antiracist, pro-LGBTQ and shaped by feminism.[8] This finding reflects recent public attitude surveys, which show that four in five Britons believe 'it is important to be alive to issues of race and social justice'[9] and that younger people have more diverse sexual and gender identifications than older age groups.[10]

This was clearest in relation to antiracism – perhaps not surprisingly given that more than half of the interviews coincided with a huge surge in racial justice activism following the murder of George Floyd. The ability to share, support and learn from #BlackLivesMatter content was mentioned spontaneously by many people I interviewed as one of the positives of their social media. Lynne, a white 19-year-old student, said 'If it weren't for Instagram, I wouldn't know half as much about #BlackLivesMatter'. Sofia, a 25-year-old student of mixed British-Greek heritage said 'it was all over TikTok and I got quite a lot of information from that that maybe wasn't in mainstream media'. Twitter, too, was:

> informative ... You have to take all of it with a grain of salt and realize that anyone could post literally anything ... But a lot of the stuff I found useful was people talking about their experiences, their perspective, where they might not necessarily previously have had a voice that I would have been able to access.

Several participants had been on the big London demonstration in support of Black Lives Matter on 31 May 2020. As one of them, Bianca, 18, who worked in a nail bar and was also hoping to go to university, talked about how crucially important social media were in breaking the story of George Floyd's murder, and in challenging mainstream media's reporting of the protests about it:

> I feel like for the Black Lives Matter movement, it's been on social media more, and the only reason why people know about it is because of social media. I went to the protest and it was peaceful. And then the media started, the news. Started saying it was violent. I was thinking: it *wasn't*. And then social media shows a different side – it's more targeted at the *police* being nasty. And it's like with George Floyd, if that wasn't caught on video, where would they have posted it without social media? So that's where it's good.

This clear personal account expresses vividly what Sarah Jackson, Moya Bailey and Brooke Foucault Welles describe as 'the importance of the digital labour of raced and gendered counterpublics'[11] centred on hashtags such as #BlackLivesMatter and #SayHerName.

Social media love, hate and ambivalence

Social media provoked markedly different feelings and experiences. A few participants expressed general huge enthusiasm for socials for the sense of community, affirmation and fun they provided: notably three interviewees (Alex, Bipasha and Ruby) told me that social media were a source of pleasure and/or support for them. By contrast, three other interviewees (Elizabeth, India, Joanne) experienced significant unhappiness in relation to social media. Most others – and indeed even these six individuals – expressed views that were ambivalent, marked by pleasure and pain, by a desire to connect but also a sense of loneliness, a wish to be seen but not to be judged. Bianca, for example, valued social media for facilitating antiracist activism ('so that's where it's good') but also recounted multiple painful experiences of being trolled and shamed on her socials for self-ies she posted. This ambivalence was even evident in the survey responses. Respondents were asked whether or not they agreed with various statements starting with: 'social media makes me feel ... attractive/confident/happy/bad about myself'. They were asked to rate each of these kinds of statements in terms of frequencies ranging from Always to Never. Because the questions were not mutually exclusive, they produced a fascinating range of answers which reveal the ambivalence experienced in relation to socials. For example, 80 per cent responded that their social media made them feel confident at least some of the time (the vast majority checked 'sometimes'). However, an identical proportion *of the same respondents* also told us that social media made them feel 'bad about yourself'. Only two questions stood out here for displaying less ambivalence: more than 90 per cent of women reported that social media made them feel 'like other people are more successful than you' and a similar proportion reported feeling 'like other people have more fun than you'.

Rather than simply categorizing individuals, it seems more productive to examine the things about social media life that people enjoyed or struggled with. Here, in fact, there was considerable consensus about what was important about social media and what might make it difficult or upsetting. The most highly valued features were friendship, community, connection, support, fun, inspiration, motivation and information. Conversely, the negative experiences were the pressures to be perfect, feeling watched, feeling judged, loneliness, addiction, depression, competition, exhaustion and feeling drained.

Managing social media lives

All the young people in this research were thoughtful, sophisticated and agentic users of social media. They made clear but subtle differentiations in their use of different platforms, different accounts, different privacy settings, and were constantly reflecting on who they followed, what they posted, and deliberating about how to align their social media presence more closely with who they felt they were or wanted to become. Many of them had used the period of lockdown to undertake a 'cleanse' of their socials to this end. As Alba, a 20-year-old white student, explained: the pandemic was one of a number of moments of change when she had gone through her social media accounts cleaning them up:

> Alba: That's changed when I've gone to uni. Again, I think it was in lockdown, I did a bit of a cleanse of people I follow, not people that follow me, but people I follow. Just that I don't really need to stay in touch with anymore. Just unfollowed those. But yes.
>
> RG: Interesting. So was that, is that celebrities or influencers that you cleared out, or is it more just people that you didn't really feel you wanted in your life anymore?
>
> Alba: Yes more just people from high school or previous schools that I wasn't, am not still in contact with or not friends with, that I just thought there's no point seeing these things anymore. And I know quite a few of my friends did that in lockdown as well when we had the time. Just had a cleanse.

Different platforms, different content, different audiences

Participants conveyed a complex but clear sense of the meaning that different platforms had for them, and the way they would use different socials for different activities, different audiences and different levels of intimacy. This is captured in the quote below from Holly who differentiates between the content she engages with and posts on the five different social media platforms she uses most:

> I mainly use Instagram. I'm active on there quite a lot. And then, obviously, I use Facebook and stuff. But I find that people our age don't really use Facebook as much. It's more of, like, a mum thing. My mum posts on Facebook every day. People my age, I don't really use Facebook that much. I'll check it every now and again, but I'm not using it every day. And then, I use Twitter quite a lot. I probably use Twitter every day, just more for following what's going on really. What people are saying, a bit of news on there, Covid stuff. Just things like that, really, that I'm just following, that I just look at. I'll probably use that every day.
>
> And then, I've started using TikTok as well . . . I don't really post on there a lot. I probably post on there every now and again. But I probably do use it every day, just watching TikToks every day. And then, obviously, there's Snapchat, as well, which I use to message my friends. I don't post much on there, but I do message. I'm part of my friends' group chats and stuff, I message people on there. So I'd probably say Instagram's the main one that I use and that I post on regularly.

Beyond this clear categorization of the meanings and uses of different socials, this research also illuminates the striking attention young women give to *managing* their various social media presences. As many prominent social media experts have discussed, this can include multiple accounts on one app. Although Meta used to consistently argue that there is only one 'real' or 'authentic' you online,[12] in practice multiple accounts are widespread. In 2016, in recognition of the proliferation of 'Finstas' (so-called fake Instagrams), Instagram added the ability to move between various different Instagram accounts, reinforced by prompts to 'Share a different side of yourself.'[13] A 20-year-old white student from Leeds, Ches, explains how she manages her three different Instagrams – one for the range of friends she has built up over her lifetime, another for her university course in design, and a third for a tighter group of friends:

> So I have my main account which is just the 1,700 people who follow me, that's friends you build up over the years, people you've known or know, just people who choose to follow you, whatever. And that's just selfies, pictures with friends, high-lights, which are from stories of nights out or whatever, but yes it's just mainly pictures, nice pictures of me and pictures of me and my friends.
>
> But then I have a separate account, I have to have for uni, so that's all design related posts, stories that are all design related. And then I have a third account, which is my private account for my close friends where I'll just post whatever I want, funny stuff, whatever, just weird things, like personal stuff.

This was a common strategy with many interviewees having multiple Instagrams that betokened different levels of intimacy and perceived freedom – as well as perhaps having a business account that could give access to various boosts and analytics, unavailable on private Instagrams. Overall, it was clear that many participants worked with some shared understandings: 'Facebook is for family', Snapchat or a private Instagram is for your close friends, and a public Instagram is where you post your 'best' pictures or videos. As Bianca, 18, put it, talking about her posting:

> It depends on what social media it is. Snapchat is mainly a video of me lip-syncing a song, I would say. Or, just a random picture of my food, or just showing them where I am, because you can put the location and it will come up. Or just funny

videos, like my friends doing something. Whereas Instagram, it's just pictures of me. So, it will be a full body picture, just showing my outfit. Or it will be a selfie, yes. And maybe the videos from Snapchat I'll post on I'll post on Instagram as well, because I have different people on there.

And then Facebook is more family I'll post, or just myself but less revealing. Got to keep it PG for the family! (laughter) And that's mostly family stuff. I wouldn't say I post a lot on there, it's just if I wanted to update my profile picture or family, a happy birthday to someone. Because they're most likely to see it on Facebook if they're older.

Time

Time was subject to intense reflection in the interviews. Participants deliberated about when to go on particular platforms, when to post and when or whether to take a break. Most of my interviewees had more time on their hands during lockdown, but were also aware that it could be wasted – as noted by India earlier in the chapter. Generally, time was something that was alternately wistfully mourned or regretted with embarrassment. Bipasha, 23, for example, laughed with a mock-shame 'oh my god, I know, it's so unhealthy' as she talked about the amount of time she spent on Instagram, while Anna, 21, expressed a mixture of shame and defiance about the number of transformation videos she had watched relating to cosmetic surgery and dentistry. Time was something that some people felt social media stole from them, conveying a sense of a theft-by-stealth that should be guarded against. Many indicted TikTok in particular for this: 'that's one I try to stay away from because you can just spend so long on it' (Nadine). Time was also something that platforms and devices reminded one of, with iPhone's announcements that 'you have a new memory' and Snapchat's anniversary feature that showed participants what they were doing a year ago, two years ago, five years ago. This was cherished by some, to the extent of becoming a reason to stick with the platform even after everything else had moved to Instagram.[14] But it could also feel like being painfully ambushed, especially if the images showed someone you no longer saw – perhaps an ex, or a friend with whom there had been a rift. However, the archiving features of their socials were loved by some. Ruby said:

> I love it! So, it's like I put it up to be like, oh, look at all the things that I'm doing. Look, this is a funny thing that I came up with. And then, partly, it's just a diary for me to go back and look at and remember the nice things that I've done.

Mistakes over timing were key worries for some. Elizabeth used only Facebook and reported that she posted a fresh profile picture one Tuesday morning at 10 AM, a few days before our interview. She then felt crushingly disappointed by the relative lack of positive appreciation, and berated herself for what she described as the 'rookie error' of her bad timing: 'I should have posted that picture on a Friday evening' she told me; it would have got far more likes. Other time-related deliberations included which photos might make the cut to move from an Instagram Story that would disappear after 24 hours, to a 'highlight' which would be there forever. It had to be something good enough, awesome enough, to merit saving in this way, yet there was a limited time in which to make the decision – and it was probably a post at night, which might involve posting by mistake or while drunk.

Night-time and early morning were the times discussed most by my participants. Lynne was one of the majority of interviewees who woke up to and with her phone every day:

> Lynne: I wake up and I check my phone. If I've got any notifica-
>   tions, I'll go straight to them. But then if it's just first thing in
>   the morning, I would just scroll through Instagram. Watch

people's stories. And then that's mostly it. I spend at least
an hour a day when I wake up, straight away, probably just
an hour on Instagram, on the explore page, or just scrolling
through. So that's pretty much it in the morning.

RG: And then are you going back to it constantly through the
day?

Lynne: Yes, I think Instagram is the one I go to the most. Not
even looking through my own ... what comes up on my
own feed, just exploring. If I have a random thought and I
think about something, I'll go to Instagram first and look up
... So, if I want to see baking or something that day then
I'll got to Instagram before I'll go to the internet. Get ideas,
whatever. Yes, so it is pretty constant throughout the day or
just checking what people are saying.

Nadine also recounts a clear diurnal pattern to her social
media use:

> Even my friends, I feel like we all very much have certain times
> that we'd go onto things. So, I feel like TikTok, if you go on that
> you try not to in the day because like we've said, you tend to
> just spend hours on it in the end. So, I tend to not go on that
> unless it's the evening, so then I can just fall asleep afterwards.
> Twitter, I always go on in the morning. I don't know how I
> got into that habit. But I feel like it's like reading the morning
> newspaper. I'll go on that in the morning.

Night-time was challenging for many participants, in
'switching off' literally and metaphorically. Nazanin told me
she tries to move her phone away from her about 30 minutes
before she wants to sleep, but said that these good intentions
are often undone by needing to pick it up again to set the
alarm. Many interviewees struggled to sleep, and were pulled
into repeatedly checking their phones late into the night. In
chapter 6, I discuss more fully the particular anxieties related

to posting at night which left many young women flooded with anxiety, and with hearts pounding for fear of having got something wrong: posted a bad photo, posted by accident, not got enough likes, etc.

Public/private/anonymous

Interviewees were roughly divided between those whose Instagrams were private – meaning they could only be seen by 'approved' followers – and those that were public – meaning they could be seen by anyone. Many people, of course, had both as I have already noted. I was struck by the thought and care that went into making such decisions. One young Black woman talked about how she had changed her account settings from private to public, with much consideration, after the death of George Floyd, as it felt important to her to make visible her support for #BlackLivesMatter, and not to keep this private. By contrast another woman – a student of Indian descent – reflected that her desire for likes and followers felt like a vestige of her younger self. She was 20 now and hoped that as she got older, she would close down her other socials and just have one private Instagram which would be accessible solely to her 'true' friends. While these strategies differ, what unites them is the thoughtfulness with which such questions were engaged.

A strikingly different approach to the public/private debate was taken by Sofia, 25, and Helena, 28, both of whom had chosen to be completely anonymous on their social media accounts. Both might – in a traditional typological approach – be characterized as 'heavy' users of social media and as social media 'enthusiasts', who said they spent hours each day on Instagram, TikTok, Twitter and YouTube, finding it amusing and in many ways pleasurable. Yet neither of them *ever posted anything, and they kept their accounts completely anonymous:* they could see what was happening but could not be seen/identified. Helena told me: 'I have Instagram but I don't have myself on it', while Sofia said: 'I use Instagram but it's like secret', and instead of a name and photo 'I have just a random number as a thing'. This way, she explained, she can participate in all the 'good stuff' but without 'making myself vulnerable' to what she characterized as 'constant judgement' and 'competition'. Nevertheless, Sofia told me she really enjoyed social media and spent many hours each day on random browsing:

> It's fun. It's funny. There's funny stuff on the internet. There is a community. There's inside jokes. It's informative, educational. I learn about stuff on Twitter five times more early than my parents learn about stuff through traditional media forums . . . And TikTok is really funny.

Sofia added: 'But I don't want to be seen'. For her, birthdays had been a painful flashpoint in the past, waiting for people 'I didn't even like' to wish me happy birthday on Facebook. Helena, by contrast had *never* had any social media accounts.

> No, I was never on any, even Myspace back in the day, I never had a Myspace, never had a Facebook, no Twitter. So just Instagram, and I can't even remember when I first made that, I think a few years ago now, but always for that purpose of just browsing without posting.

She explained that the 'exhaustion' of having to create and maintain an 'unreal' and 'perfect' 'persona' made her uncomfortable, as well as fearful of 'who would be able to see it'. 'So I think it was both I liked preserving my anonymity, and it was too much effort, it felt like a lot of effort to create and maintain a social media presence.' She also worried about becoming dependent upon it for validation of her worth, recognizing that this was a matter of struggle for her:

Because I have a tendency to seek validation from lots of places already, and I didn't want social media to become another one of those places. And I didn't want to become addicted and dependent on my interactions on social media, I was very aware that that could be a very slippery slope for me. So that was another reason I think I was very hesitant to join, and still am.

One other participant who was also a social media enthusiast, and who had garnered 85,000 followers across Instagram and TikTok for her modest fashion posts was Ayeshah. Extraordinarily – given her success as a micro-influencer – Ayeshah also remained anonymous on her public Instagram. She posted frequently but did not show her face or use her name. As well as wearing a hijab, she described how she cropped her photos to remove her face, or she turned away, or artfully used her hands to cover her face. She told me this anonymity gave her a degree of freedom and emotional protection, meaning that when she received negative comments, she would not dwell on them, but would simply 'block the account' they came from. This experience stood in stark contrast to other participants whose identity was known, even if on a relatively private account, who described significant distress at hostile comments (as discussed later in the book).

Conclusion

This chapter has explored the huge variety of ways in which young women and nonbinary people live life on their phones. It has foregrounded the active, thoughtful and deliberative approaches that young people use to engage with which platforms to be on, who or what to follow, whether to have settings on public or private, and myriad other issues. It has also looked at the emotional textures of social media lives, pointing to

some differences in participants' affective orientations to their
socials – that ranged from love to hate – but prioritizing an
understanding that stresses both the widespread ambivalence
experienced, and the extent to which most of the pleasures
and pains were experienced by all to some degree. In the next
chapter I look at how this critical and reflective stance came up
against the ubiquitous emphasis upon being 'perfect'.

2

Picture perfect:
The power of images

Why don't I look like the people I see on social media? . . . I feel like I'll never be good enough (Ayeshah, 20)

People aren't happy all the time or beautiful all the time. Despite pores being something everyone has on their face, we very rarely see them . . . There are so many different aspects to the unrealistic images. . . . It is all so airbrushed and perfect and happy. (Comment left on survey)

If I were to single out one phrase that I heard more than any other while doing this research, it would be 'it's all too perfect'. As young women talked about their lives on social media, the topic of perfection came up again and again. Perhaps not surprisingly, celebrities and influencers were frequently indicted as 'too perfect', always looking beautiful, photographed in stunning locations, with incredible food and drinks, and alongside other 'shiny, happy people' who appeared effortlessly cool and good-looking. This motif has become the well-recognized cliché of Instagram perfection, yet it still has the power to cause distress. More than this, however, young women told me that their peers' and friends' posts and stories were also often intimidatingly perfect. Young women recounted that as they scroll through the feeds on their phones it often feels as if everyone is more attractive than them, and everyone is doing better than them in their jobs, relationships or studies. It looks like 'everyone else is having such a great time' and 'living these perfect lives' and that can be 'very difficult'.

There is nothing new about media representations of 'perfect' female bodies. Women's bodies have long been presented in idealized, sexualized or objectified ways – in paintings, in advertising, in music videos – and this has been a topic of feminist research for decades.[1] Today, however, the *sheer number* of images of women's bodies surpasses anything that has gone before. Visual culture is expanding, accelerating and amplifying, and images are proliferating at a rate that is difficult to grasp. Only a few years ago media scholars used to attempt to quantify how long 'the average person' would spend looking at or engaging with media, for example how many advertising images they might typically encounter in a day. The advent of social media challenged such endeavours. Quickly historians began to produce striking new statistics – highlighting, for example, that there have been more new images produced in the twenty-first century than in the entirety of human history preceding that. But today even such powerful and hyperbolic attempts to show the scale of our image-based world cannot keep pace. According to Phototutorial,[2] 1.72 *trillion* photographs were taken in 2022, which equates to 4.7 *billion* per day. On Instagram alone, 1.3 billion photographs or videos are posted every single day. Everyday life has become utterly saturated by visuality, in a way that has no historical precedent and leaves researchers struggling to make sense of what it means – particularly when so many of the images that we see are carefully curated, augmented and manipulated to look 'perfect'.

Young women often struggle with this image-based media culture, which disproportionately focuses on women's bodies. They are aware that it is not 'real', and they talked in detail about the techniques that produce the curated perfection they see on their socials. What's more, their skills at managing social media lives, discussed in the previous chapter, are enhanced by the probing and critical questions they ask about much that they look at, such as 'who made this image?', 'what is it trying to sell me?', 'is it authentic?' and 'has it been filtered or edited?'. Far from being passively subjugated by images of female perfection, then, young women are eloquent analysts and critics of the images they engage with and produce. They demonstrate a sophisticated understanding of the scale and force of images of perfect appearance, and also the patterns and exclusions of these images – their overwhelming whiteness, heteronormativity, slimness, etc. Nevertheless, as I show in this chapter, despite young women's articulate critiques, they feel caught and trapped by the ubiquitous representation of bodily perfection; *they may be angry about it, but they also feel they have to live up to it.* They do not operate outside its powerful force and their critiques do not facilitate the ability to escape the tyranny of the perfect.

The chapter makes three main arguments that relate to: the power of perfect images, the pain of the perfect and the politics of the perfect. In the first section of the chapter, I explore young women's experiences of social media lives dominated by perfect aesthetics. I discuss what they told me about feeling that they had spent their lives being trained or tutored into an impossible ideal of femininity. I consider their experiences of constantly comparing themselves with others, and I present their sobering accounts of the anxiety, shame and self-contempt they experience as they encounter streams of perfect images of women's bodies and faces. In the second part, I consider their intersectional critiques of the perfect, highlighting the way in which the very meaning of the perfect is shaped by assumptions about race, class, sexuality, body size, disability and health. Finally, I look briefly at young women's feminist criticisms of their social media feeds, their interest in body positivity and their sense that things are changing. But I show that, despite their articulate critiques, they still feel caught by the requirement to be 'perfect'.

The power of the image

The pressure to be perfect is about more than looking attractive. It has, as cultural theorist Angela McRobbie has put it, become a 'horizon of expectation'[3] for young women across multiple aspects of their lives, in a context in which patriarchy is said to have 'reterritorialized in the fashion-beauty complex'.[4] Perfection is imbued with the status of a 'moral imperative',[5] with the requirement to 'be living your best life at all times', as several young women put it. It is about being seen to be cool, popular, positive, authentic and relatable. But in an image-based social media culture, *looking good* is central to this. In the survey the full 100 per cent of female respondents agreed that society places significant importance on appearance, and in the free answers and in extensive discussions in interviews they shared how they experienced this. The pressure is 'overwhelming' said many respondents. Others confessed 'we feel bombarded'. A sense of the *impossibility* of this pulsed through young women's accounts. It made them feel anxious, ashamed and like they will never be good enough, they told me.

Time after time young women reported that the images of women they see every day are 'too perfect', showing 'ideals' of appearance that are 'unrealistic' and 'unachievable'. 'Tall, thin, perfect – it's so unrealistic', said one young woman. 'Visually perfect', said another. 'Way too perfect' and 'skinny, airbrushed, perfect-looking', said others. 'They have been filtered and photoshopped to death'.

There was a high degree of consensus around the increasing importance of looks to representations of women across all media. As one respondent put it, 'I think women are represented as beautiful people. I think media focuses more on appearance than what they do.' Another said: 'Women are judged more than men on the way they look, the media often portrays women's value to be in their looks.' Others noted that the women they see pictured are 'almost always gorgeous with blemish-free skin and long, thick hair'. In the free comments on the survey, someone else wrote:

> Their (sic) represented in a way that tells the world that every woman should have the following: Shiny hair, bright eyes, big lips, clear skin, just enough boob to have cleavage, flat stomachs, thigh gaps, peachy or big bums, long and painted nails and dainty feet. So basically like sex objects that men want to have sex with or 'the perfect woman' Its not always like this but I'd say 8/10 (spelling and punctuation from original).

Learning to be perfect

A sense of the ubiquitous pressure of the perfect body and perfect appearance was often the first thing that anyone talked about in relation to social media, particularly Instagram. The encounter with perfect images was one of the most powerful memories that participants recounted of getting social media as children or teens. Ayeshah, 20, a Black, Muslim Londoner, who was a student at the time of her interview, had really wanted to get Instagram in her early teens but was not allowed to, and consequently felt as if everyone at her school had it before her. When she finally got an account aged 15, however, she told me – as so many others also did – that she immediately started questioning herself and feeling bad. She said she asked herself:

> Why don't I look like that, why don't I look like this person on social media? Or what can I change to make myself more appealing to other people? And I think that, growing up, I had

huge insecurities, just because everyone was trying to make themselves look like people on social media. And I felt like there weren't a lot of people on social media that looked like me. I struggled with that. I had really deep insecurity issues. And especially because I went to a girls school for five years and that kind of environment was very much like heavy on social media and looking a certain way . . . Perfect skin. Perfect hair. The perfect body . . . And I remember there was a trend of having thick eyebrows and thick lips as well . . . People would make comments all the time. I felt a huge pressure to look a certain way.

As Ayeshah explains, she did not see many young women who looked like her on Instagram at the time – a brown-skinned woman who wore a hijab – which left her with a sense of insecurity and of not feeling right. It was painful to hear her describe how she tried to change herself to fit in. She also expressed vividly how these pressures came not only from the platform itself but from the social relations in which Instagram was embedded in her school. Instead of offering a respite from, or resistance to, the pressures of the perfect, her peer networks animated and reinforced the pressures with constant comments and assessments about how much each girl conformed or not to current beauty standards of who had the best eyebrows or nicest-shaped mouth. She regarded her school years on Instagram as a period in which she was tutored into norms of desirable 'perfect' femininity – how to smile, how to hold your body for a photograph, how to dress, how to make up your face, how to make your eyebrows into the currently fashionable shape. This emphasis on learning is found in a growing body of work on social media as pedagogical institutions, as I discuss more fully in chapter 3.

Never good enough: endless comparison

Ayeshah's account of her teen years on Instagram also brings an emphasis upon comparison – on and off social media – much discussed in psychological research. This was extensively discussed by others too. 'It feels like women are just there to be looked at and compared to each other', someone wrote on the survey. India, a 21-year-old from the Midlands, said her primary experience of Instagram was of appearance pressure through comparisons with peers:

> It's all too perfect again. Yes. Skin condition and all these adverts of perfect skin, perfect eyebrows, all of that kind of thing . . . If you're not looking like that, you just think, why am I not looking like that? How do they even look like that? Yes. Just general health things . . . You just think, it can't be that difficult. They all look amazing and I don't look like that. So definitely there's a, this is what you must look like.

Likewise, Lily, a white student, formerly from Poland but now living in Belfast, said that she was *always* comparing herself to others she sees on social media – not just influencers and celebrities, but her friends as well: 'And that's quite upsetting. And it's just that comparison, that constant comparison to people. And sometimes it can be quite draining.' What made it particularly difficult, several participants explained, was that the images of perfect appearance weren't just distant film stars or celebrities with great wealth and teams of people whose job it was to make them look good, but rather were their peers. The most painful comparisons were not with Kardashians or Jenners or Hollywood actresses, but other young women like them. Emma told me that her social media feeds were full of people she knows who 'look better than the best I've ever looked', underscoring the force of comparison as a dynamic.

Tanisha, a 26-year-old Black woman currently studying in London, extended the discussion of comparison with peers to include other features, describing how, a few months before our interview, she had been feeling 'really down', and how this was exacerbated by seeing her friends and former classmates posting:

I was seeing people I went to college with were like graduating from law school, graduating from med school, or they just got promoted. And I was like, oh my goodness, everyone is successful but me. I really definitely felt that. I was, like, wow . . . Wow I'm so far behind. So that was a period when I really felt down looking at social media.

She went on to explain that:

Now I feel that a lot of my peers they're like getting married, or they're married and they're having kids . . . and I look at it and I'm like oh wow am I behind? Am I doing something wrong? I don't know.

Difficult but dynamic feelings

As the quotes from Tanisha, Lily, Emma, Ayeshah, India and others make clear, social media dominated by perfect images was experienced as difficult by many young women. It is associated with feelings of insecurity (Ayeshah), of exhaustion and fatigue (Lily), of depression (Lily) and of feeling behind (Tanisha), wrong (Letitia) and not good enough (India). Alongside and entangled within these feelings, as they were described by young women, was a strong current of shame that is discussed throughout this book. Cultural theorist Sara Ahmed calls shame a 'sticky' emotion, which can attach easily to some people or bodies more than others, particularly those that are already accorded less value because of their size, ability, ethnicity or gender.[6] It also, as Sally Munt explains, 'tends to leave a residue to which other emotions are easily attached, namely envy, hate, contempt, apathy, painful self-absorption, humiliation, rage, mortification and disgust'.[7]

Many of these feelings were evident across the interviews, but what was also striking was the dynamism of young women's accounts and experiences. That is, images of perfection could be experienced on one occasion as inspiring and motivating, but on another as overwhelming, shaming and leading to a sense of despair. Tanisha explained this vividly as she talked about the effects on her of seeing so many perfect images on her socials:

> A little bit of it is motivating, because then I think oh, like, you know, let me dress up today or let me do my hair, let me put on makeup, but, yes, most of the time I'm just like, oh no, let me not look at it, it's too much. It's too much pressure.

She told me that as she had got older, she had become better at recognizing when the difficult feelings were going to get overwhelming, and realizing that she needs to 'take a break', otherwise she will start to feel 'really down'.

Letitia too recounted how the same images could generate different feelings, depending on her mood or confidence on a particular day:

> So, sometimes I see stuff, and I'm like, oh, this is amazing. I feel great. And then, sometimes, it's like stick thin women with the most amazing butt and the most amazing long hair, and I'm just like, this isn't me, and why am I constantly seeing this? And it does make you feel abnormal, sometimes, and you *are* normal. Like, every shape and every size and . . .
>
> Even when it comes to my skin, I know in my head that is normal. But when you see the content, it's like, it does make you feel almost *abnormal* because it's showing you that it shouldn't

be that way and that *that's* what you should look like. So, for me, I have a love-hate relationship with it because sometimes I do feel really inspired, and sometimes I'm just, oh, I *hate you*. It's really up and down.

As Letitia concluded this thoughtful reflection, she was emphatic in articulating the hate she can sometimes feel for social media, for making her feel bad, even 'abnormal'. At a later point in the interview, she recounted a similarly powerful emotion, saying she sometimes feels 'oh go away' – and she used her hands to mime repeatedly pushing away the painful feelings that are generated by perfect images on her socials. What both Tanisha's and Letitia's accounts show, beyond the mix of pleasure and distress, inspiration and pressure, they experience on their social media, is their *critical orientation* – they *know* that their bodies, their skin, their hair *'are normal'* (to use Letitia's words), but, despite this, they still experience feeling 'really down' or 'abnormal' because of the photos they see all the time. Knowing the images are fake, manipulated or being critical of them for another reason does not erase their affective or emotional force. This is the experience of being critical, yet still feeling caught or pressured. It is a complicated and seemingly contradictory dynamic that is based in articulate critiques of the tyranny of perfect images, alongside the desire to look just like them; it facilitates eloquent criticism of social media as shame-making apparatuses, yet also generates ugly feelings[8] of shame. Moreover, to add a further twist, young women also demonstrate an awareness of precisely this dynamic – they reflect critically on the very experience of being trapped. As one commenter wrote on the survey about media generally:

In most media women's bodies are slim, toned, tanned and hairless. This is not realistic for me or most women i know, yet the media still tells us that the reason our bodies do not look like this ideal type is because we haven't worked hard for it yet. This allows companies to sell products to us which promise to help improve our flaws, flaws which would not be considered a flaw in the first place had it not been for the media telling us it is so.

The dynamic of articulating a powerful – often feminist – critique of social media images, but then expressing distress about how those images made one feel was a striking feature of the interviews, even when, as in this example, there is also an additional meta-critique of this very process of being made to feel flawed or a failure. There seemed to be no 'escape' as this comment on the survey captures vividly:

> There is still a certain kind of unwritten expectation. You SHOULD be slimmer, have shiny hair and white skin, wear makeup, go to gym, dress up and stay young and attractive. It makes me feel upset when I find that no matter how high socioeconomic women have, how high reputation women own, they still cannot escape from that expectation.

The perfect: an intersectional analysis

So far I have looked at young women's experiences of perfect social media images and how they made them feel. But the perfect is not only an aesthetic or evaluative category; it is also racialized, classed, gendered and shaped by assumptions about disability, sexuality and skin colour.[9] Many participants were articulate in commenting on the implicit assumptions and exclusions in the images that they see on social media. As one person wrote on the survey:

> Most influencers on social media are slim, blonde and tan – which yes a lot of people are but it creates this idea that

that's what you SHOULD look like. Also the racial diversity is AWFUL as they only depict one sort of image that people should conform to (spelling and capitalization from original)

Others said variously: 'everyone looks the same', 'there is a distinct lack of diversity' and 'most women portrayed are skinny, white and straight'. Often the force of this was framed in terms of personal experiences, as I discuss below.

The whiteness and lightness of media

A strong motif in both the interviews and the responses to the survey centred on the whiteness of both mainstream or legacy media (such as film, television and print journalism) and social media – reflecting the entrenched whiteness of many media companies and tech giants. For many participants this exacerbated long and deeply held experiences of not feeling represented. As one woman put it in a thoughtful response to the question about whether media representations reflect your life: 'As a Black woman the media rarely represent us so it's hard for me to see myself in that aspect.' Another woman told me: 'I am Sri Lankan British and I haven't heard of any major characters of similar origin' throughout my life. Someone else reported 'As someone of mixed White/East Asian ethnicity growing up in England, I did not see anyone really representing myself in the television I watched or the magazines I read.'

Young people of diverse racial and ethnic backgrounds reported the devastating impact that not seeing anyone like themselves in media had upon their sense of self. 'It massively affects my self-confidence', one young Black woman said in an interview. Another, of south Asian heritage, said it had made it very difficult to 'relate ... as very few south Asian women are represented positively in the media'. Tanisha commented critically on platforms' algorithms, which repeatedly offered her *white images* of the beauty trends she followed:

So I definitely noticed it seems like anything you search, if you basically want to see a non-white face you have to alter your search parameters ... say minimal makeup ... it's all white creators. You don't see other creators unless you scroll, scroll, scroll, or you specifically type, like, clean girl make up *Black girl*.

Tanisha was particularly critical of TikTok in this respect, highlighting the algorithmic oppression and injustice that is increasingly widely discussed.[10]

Exclusions and invisibility were not the only issues. For many Black women there was a contradictory reality of both *invisibility and hyper-visibility*[11] in which, when they saw themselves represented, it was in a narrow range of 'hyper-sexualized' ways.[12] As one young Black woman put it: 'It's all sex sex sex appeal girls with big bum, big boobs, slim thick, long thick hair, it's all fake girls these days.' This reflects the pervasiveness of the sexual commodification of Black women's bodies, and prominent contemporary constructions of sexualized and racialized 'hotness'.[13] Safiya Noble's powerful critique of algorithmic injustice highlights the racialized sexualization that young Black women are subject to, arguing that it has been 'engineered in' to search engines that repeatedly offer pornographic results for word searches on 'Black girls'.[14] The prevalence of these kinds of representations had material effects on young Black women – for example in terms of negative judgements made of them (such as the slut-shaming they receive) and their personal safety, an issue discussed later in the book.

Participants of all ethnicities commented upon shifting body and beauty standards, and particularly the trend for bigger and more curvy bodies, which was welcomed as part of wider trends to greater 'body positivity'. There was a sense that ideals were changing and that several distinctive versions of 'the perfect' were circulating and co-existing, most notably a white, slim, blonde Californian aesthetic, alongside a racially ambiguous – or perhaps 'racially mobile'[15] – 'slim-thick' model.

However, a consistent feature of such ideals, young women told me, was their valuing of lighter skin, reflecting the prominence of colourism, 'prejudice on the basis of skin shade'.[16] The troubling media practice of lightening the skins of celebrities of colour for magazine shoots or publicity shots – for example Beyonce and Lupita Nyong'o – alongside recent revelations about how skin shade affects the fees received by influencers, find their counterpart in what many young Black women characterized as a systematic privileging of lighter skin on social media platforms. Adija, 27, who was of mixed white British and Nigerian heritage, commented that when she auditions for roles as a dancer or performer in theatre and advertising, it is often 'only mixed race girls and I look exactly like everyone else on the panel'. The finding supports Aisha Phoenix's analysis of magazines, cosmetic surgery sites, Twitter posts and media culture more broadly, demonstrating the 'symbolic violence' of colourism and its relation to racism and sexism.[17]

Intimately related to this is what some experienced as a *cultural appropriation of blackness* as central to contemporary appearance ideals. A compelling argument was made by Sofia, 25, who was Greek-British and unemployed after recently graduating:

> I blame it all on the Kardashians (laughter). It's all their fault. There's a very certain look ... The Instagram look in a lot of ways actually is more like the Black beauty standard but it's only on white people. So they want to have that curvaceous, skinny, skinny legs, massive bum, tiny waist, maybe not big boobs, they're not that in now actually. A little bit of something. Big lips. Small nose. Very very that. Tanned. Very racially ambiguous I would say ... And it's quite *appropriative* I would say and that's why I blame it on the Kardashians.

Sofia's analysis resonates with contemporary writing about 'Blackfishing', which Wanna Thompson has argued refers to the way that white influencers appropriate the hairstyles, 'glow' and other aspects of African American (or in UK context African Caribbean) identity as something that can be taken on or off at will, like a kind of 'digital Blackface'. Thompson argues

> In recent years, Instagram has become a breeding ground for white women who wish to capitalize off of impersonating racially ambiguous/Black women for monetary and social gain. With extensive lip fillers, dark tans and attempts to manipulate their hair texture, white women wear Black women's features like a costume. These are the same features that, once derided by mainstream white culture, are now coveted and dictate current beauty and fashion on social media, with Black women's contributions being erased all the while.[18]

Alongside forceful points about cultural appropriation is a dual critique about presenting as Black while not having to deal with the 'consequences of Blackness' in a racist world, and the possibilities of 'Being Black for a Day'[19] while undermining and erasing Black women themselves.

Gender and sexuality

Some parallel dynamics were seen in relation to gender and sexuality and the pressure to be perfect. Participants who identified as LGBTQ+ often reported that social media platforms as a whole – outside their specific communities – were steeped in heteronormative values. 'Rarely do I see someone that I identify with', said one participant, saying that there seemed little interest in 'portraying LGBTQ+ people accurately'. One lesbian woman said that the frames and assumptions of social media do not reflect her life: 'Women are so often presented in relation to men (as a wife, girlfriend, sex object or in a heterosexual family), so as a lesbian woman I don't relate to these images.' Another opined that as 'a young, conventionally attractive white woman I am able to see aspects of myself in media' but that this is partial: 'my life as a queer person in a queer relationship with a less than perfect family relationship is not often represented'.

Lesbian, bisexual and queer women found their own desires, relationships and styles of self-presentation invisibilized. They described feeling largely invisible across media as a whole, and having had hardly any opportunities to see anyone like them while they were in their teens. Indeed, a small handful of individual films and TV shows were repeatedly highlighted as crucial to the experience of growing up queer, with *Glee*'s Brittany and Santana relationship mentioned as especially significant,[20] partly because it was one of so few storylines that featured a lesbian relationship. Helena, 28, said

> As a non-straight women I remember when I was a teenager and there were even fewer representations. So I have to admit it does make me happy that there are more representations [now], but they're still generally white, they're not that diverse ... My issue with those representations is that they're often very one-dimensional and very exploitatively used often. And it is patronizing but also works because there are no other representations, so it works to get an audience.

As in relation to race, invisibility was exacerbated by other issues, some of which are hinted at by Helena here. One was the perception that the increase in representations of LGBTQ+ people had been dominated by gay men, leaving women to contend with a generalized sense that things have 'got better', but one with which they did not necessarily identify. 'There's still a long way to go', more than one queer woman told me. During the course of the research, Russell T. Davies's acclaimed drama *It's a Sin*, about the AIDS crisis in the eighties, had aired on

Channel 4, generating some discussion of its alleged erasure of women and particularly lesbians. *Drag Race* has also popularized a particular version of gay male culture, which one lesbian participant described as 'a double-edged sword for LGBTQ+ people'.

The 'bury your gays' trope, in which, notoriously, queer characters are 'killed off' in dramas, was also felt to impact women disproportionately, with one participant discussing the sense of dread she felt whenever a gay woman character was introduced in a TV series, wondering 'how long she's going to last'. Storylines were often experienced as 'thin', 'one-dimensional' and 'unsatisfying'. Finally, several queer participants were angered by the highly sexualized portrayal of queer women that seemed designed to satisfy a heterosexual male gaze. This was easy to distinguish from authentic representations, participants suggested, as 'it is often quite gratuitous . . . two femme women who have never shown any sexual interest in women will suddenly be pictured making out on a dancefloor'. 'That stuff still happens', Helena reported, arguing that it forms the context in/against which all non-straight women have to fashion a way to exist.

Despite the gradual increase in visibility of transgender people in the media since 2014, and the increasing awareness of the numbers of people who identify outside a rigid gender binary, gender nonconforming people also felt invisible, outside of specific LGBTQ+ or trans communities online. One person said: 'Given how binary gender roles and their portrayals are, portraying nonbinary folks like me is seemingly impossible, because everyone assumes I'm either "man" or "woman".' Another person simply wrote on the survey open answers: 'There are hardly any media representations I can relate to as a nonbinary person.' A further response suggested that even the very rare representations are themselves highly problematic: 'If our existence is not being questioned to fuck, then we are shown as sad, confused, maybe even a bit dangerous people.'

In an interview Alex, who was white, nonbinary and 20 years old, elaborated how painful this invisibility could feel, rendering them 'unreadable' or 'unidentifiable' in what they felt to be a central sense of their identity. Indeed, they mention a 'defining moment' in which they saw a minor character on the TV show *New Amsterdam* identified as nonbinary.[21]

> RG: You mentioned the almost complete invisibility of nonbinary people in mainstream media. Are there any examples that you can think of?
>
> Alex: Yes. I can think of . . . I'm watching a show called *New Amsterdam* and there's a nurse in that who goes by they/them pronouns. They are not a big character. They're just in the background sometimes but they're referred to with they/them pronouns and they have a little badge on their lanyard that says, they/them. That was just a really nice thing to see. Like, cool.

Alex also explains that while there are representations of nonbinary people on the trans-supportive sites that they follow, most of the people participating are young. One of the consequences of this is it makes it difficult to imagine themselves growing older – they lack any role models and experience it as:

> really difficult to imagine my future because if everyone you see who's like you is young, it's hard to imagine growing up.
>
> Because if you don't see any grownup nonbinary people, you're like what does my future even look like? I know that I'm still going to be nonbinary in the future but what would that look like? I think that's something that has been, for me . . . I've been trying to seek out.

Disability, health and illness

Notions of the perfect are profoundly shaped by pervasive disablism. This operates to invisibilize disabled people – as one woman wrote on the survey, 'Women with disabilities are rarely shown.' But even more fundamentally than this invisibility was the experience of feeling that the *very category of 'perfect' constitutively excludes* people with disabilities. This had a profound impact on disabled participants, who reported high levels of unhappiness and depression. Of the ten disabled women who participated in the research, seven said that they felt that 'my body and appearance will never be good enough', while more than half said that they felt 'depressed' and a similar proportion said they had no self-confidence. Soberingly, nine disagreed or strongly disagreed with the statement 'I would not change my appearance or body.'

One disabled interviewee, Katie, said she felt 'invisible' and she described herself as a person who is 'hidden' from view. She eloquently discussed being caught between her personal media 'communities' – especially on Facebook – for people with the same condition as her, where she found some support but which she sometimes experienced as depressing and overwhelming – and wider media culture where she never saw anyone like her. As a 20-year-old student, with a condition similar to multiple sclerosis whose flare-ups often mean using crutches or a wheelchair, she said when she looks at clothes or fashion on social media:

> there's not really anywhere that has disabled people. And that's really difficult because it's like oh, this clothing looks really good on you, but you're all standing up. So what's it going to look like if I'm in my wheelchair.

One result of this was that she struggled to know how to present herself on social media sites in which everyone seemed to be beautiful, happy and non-disabled.

> Yes. I think I'm a hidden person. So, I feel like social media is just too personal and too open. Even with my medical condi-

tions, I would purposefully ... I can't say that. Purposefully hide ... Yes, I wouldn't show my medical conditions and stuff like that online. If there was a photo of me on crutches, I'd crop them out ... I guess it's just a confidence thing. And people, now, are so judgemental, especially on social media. It's always like a comparison of who's got things the best.

Representations of illness and of mental health issues were also seen as problematic by several participants. 'There's not much correct representation of people with mental health problems', said one survey respondent. As I noted in the Introduction, reflecting the high incidence of mental health challenges among this demographic, many participants identified as having mental health issues of varying degrees of severity. These included two interviewees – and several survey respondents – who were recovering/had recovered from eating disorders, participants who had been diagnosed with OCD, ADHD, autism spectrum disorders, and numerous participants who suffered from anxiety, depression or social anxiety. Nazanin, 18, said: 'you get some Instagram feeds that are quite positive like self-help, and how to support a friend who might be struggling, or how to take time out for yourself if you're struggling', but there's also 'a toxic dark side to it where it is very easy for someone who may be struggling to be drawn into something very negative without them going too far out of their way' – such as Pro-Ana sites or suicide sites.[22] Eve, 21, discussed having suffered from severe anorexia when she was 14 and 15, and believed – echoing Ayeshah's experience discussed earlier in the chapter – that it was not a coincidence that this was when she started using Instagram. She said:

I don't want to be all doom and gloom, but ... I think social media 100% influenced that ... I was following all these accounts where it was models, influencers, and just people who would be 100% editing their photos. Whereas now I only really follow people I know, I don't really follow influencer or model accounts, maybe that's helped subconsciously.

The topic of how 'open' one could be about any of these conditions on social media was contested. On the one hand, there was some consensus that mental health could be talked about more freely today, especially with influencers and celebrities regularly 'coming out' about their mental health challenges through posts on Instagram. On the other, for an 'ordinary person' to talk about such issues could often generate censure and accusations of being 'attention seeking'; it does not fit the 'perfect' presentation required. This is an issue I return to later in the book.

Class, wealth and body size

Another way in which participants experienced the impossibility of 'perfect' social media images was in relation to issues of class, money and time. For some young women, speaking during the context of the pandemic and the cost-of-living crisis, these images were far beyond reach and served to make them feel angry or depressed. The following comments were all left on the survey:

> Social media presents people who are always achieving – always working out, starting businesses and wearing nice clothes. It's not only that I – or many people I know – couldn't afford this lifestyle, it's just that it's impossible to be achieving all the time.

> They have more money than the average person, bigger house, etc.

> Portrayals of students and low income demographics are confined to stereotypes.

I don't have the time to look like people I see in the media . . .
It makes me feel angry because we all internalize it though as
being normal.

In the interviews too the focus on the consumption of
expensive foods, clothes and makeup brands was experienced
as alienating, with comments about not having 'the money to
buy things like that'. It could produce feelings of shame about
young women's own foods, clothes, bedrooms, etc., which
could be experienced as 'not good enough'.[23] This resonates
with Christina Scharff's analysis of how class background may
affect who feels 'at ease' – comfortable and confident – 'in
producing visually engaging content'.[24]

Body shape and size were also key to young women's sense
of identity, and participants described horrible experiences of
fat-shaming, as well as disturbing levels of self-hatred. Joanne,
23, a painter and decorator from Wales, told me:

I did struggle with moving up a clothes size [during the pan-
demic] . . . and there are some parts of my body that I'm always
going to dislike and are never going to change no matter how
much I want to improve on them. I'm always going to have
stretch marks now. It's just a given.

Joanne talked in the interview about feeling unlovable, and
how, although she tries hard to accept herself, she doesn't
believe that anyone else would want to be with her. She said
she was 'not very body confident' concluding painfully that
she knows 'no one else could think worse [of me] than what I
would think [of myself]'.

The anguish behind these words was hard to hear, but far
from unique. Letitia, 27, told me: 'some days it is like your
feed is *punishing* you, coming up with these tiny women in
swimsuits'. The words 'skinny' and 'slim' were used repeatedly
to describe the vast majority of social media representations

of women. Many respondents told me 'my body type is almost never represented in the media'. Many more talked about editing their photos in such a way as to make them appear slimmer. One young woman described how she has to undertake a huge amount of psychological work on herself just to feel 'ok' about her size in a social media universe that is so obsessed with women's weight. She said she longed to be slim and had been deeply unhappy throughout her time at school, but realized that 'if I keep hating myself cos of trends I'm going to hate myself forever'.

Critical takes

It should be clear from the argument presented so far that young people are far from cultural dupes, passively subjugated by social media's ideals of perfection. On the contrary they are articulate analysts of social media trends, and offer compelling critiques of the images they encounter and produce. Many participants had a feminist sensibility, and, as I have shown, some offered extremely sophisticated analyses that addressed not only gender inequality but intersecting oppressions related to race, disability, class, neurodiversity and sexual orientation. Indeed, several dazzlingly perceptive feminist analyses, left on the free comments section of the survey, would not have felt out of place on a graduate feminist media studies programme. They ranged over issues of exclusion and erasure, hypervisibility, sexualization, economic injustice, commodification and appropriation, often with examples from across television, popular music, advertising and other forms. One read:

I'm a feminist (trans-inclusive, intersectionality-focussed) so with this lens I see a lot of representation of women in media is super iffy; it can be objectifying, commodifying, patronizing, infantilizing, sexualizing, invasive and creepy in general. Lots of social pressures around looks, body size etc (lookism and fat phobia), needing to conform, erasure of disability/neuro-diversity etc. racism is a big issue, white supremacist beauty standards are ever present, cisheteronormativity is assumed in every portrayal. Media and women is often a trash garbage fire to be honest.

Wow! Elizabeth, 23, too, spoke eloquently about her feminism, and was articulate in her anger about the deliberate manipulation of women's body insecurities, and the connection of this to capitalist media and beauty industries deliberately profiting from this:

I just think all of this stuff is wrong. A thing which makes me really angry actually, is how we're fed so many images of people that aren't real, and all it does is to serve to make us feel insecure about ourselves.

And I feel like that insecurity is necessary for the kind of capitalist society that we live in, where it's all about increasing consumption and things, because it means that people feel sad about themselves so they buy things to make themselves feel better, or they buy beauty products to make themselves look better.

Beyond these thoughtful and insightful analyses there was a more widely shared orientation that was redolent of what Sarah Banet-Weiser has characterized as 'popular feminism'[25] and Catherine Rottenberg as 'neoliberal feminism'[26] and that I have written about as a postfeminist sensibility.[27] The contours of this orientation are distinctive in their focus upon the individual and individualism as core; an emphasis on working on the self and self-optimization as engines of change; in their attention to issues of visibility and culture; and in their concern with psychological dispositions including confidence, resilience, self-love and positivity. Such emphases were widespread among many participants, whose feminist lexicon centred around bodily autonomy; resistance to judging or being judged; sexual freedoms and antipathy to censorship; the celebration of 'empowerment'; and an orientation to self-love, self-care and pride. These orientations materialized in discussions of cosmetic surgery, in anger about shadow banning, and, perhaps above all, in the centring of 'body positivity' as at the heart of many participants' feminism. I will return to some of the complexities of body positivity in the final chapter of the book.

Conclusion: the costs of the perfect

In this chapter I have examined what young women told me was a requirement – to appear 'perfect' at all times – on social media, documenting how this was learned and intensified through comparisons with others. Although beauty standards are not fixed and do change – as seen in the way that a 'slim-thick' ideal is identified as co-existing with a tall, slim, blonde aesthetic and also, arguably, with the resurgence of super-skinny waif-like models – the chapter highlighted the many ways in which assumptions about race, sexuality and disability are 'built into' and constitutive of the very notion of the perfect. The chapter also showed that for many participants the perfect was intimately entangled with 'ugly feelings'[28] centred on depression, shame and sometimes despair. Young women told me repeatedly 'I feel like I will never be good enough' and 'I always feel bad about my body and face' and 'It has destroyed my confidence'. They expressed their anger at the 'impossibility of it'; they spoke of their worry about younger sisters, cousins and in one case children they babysit, for whom they think it will be even worse; and their voices cracked as they spoke of the hurt this causes them personally and how being critical of it does not make it go away. Letitia is passionately committed to antiracist, feminist and body positive movements, yet explains how the pressure is always there, even when you are trying hard not to let it get to you:

And even when you say, oh, I'm fine, that doesn't bother me, in the back of your mind, it is still like, well, everyone else on Instagram looks this way. And the content is telling you you should look this way, and I look like this. It's just a bit . . . It can put you down when you're not in the greatest of moods, and when that narrative is pushed.

In the next chapter I look at how the beauty industry – now experienced via the phone – is deliberately exacerbating such pressures and creating new ways of seeing.

3

The beauty industry on my phone

It's been coming up on my page . . . I get quite a lot on my Instagram . . . get bigger lips, get more cheekbones in here, and an eyebrow lift. And the fact that I even know about this, it's just bad. (Lily, 20)

Young women's experiences of the pressures of living up to perfect images is shaped by the omnipresence of a beauty industry, which has expanded so much that it no longer makes sense – if it ever did – to think of it as a singular entity. While the words 'beauty industry' may call to mind high street salons offering skin treatments, or upmarket clinics where white-coated staff perform surgeries, in practice most women now encounter the beauty industry via their phones. And they encounter it all the time. It is seen in Get Ready With Me videos, transformation challenges, before and after videos, in photo-editing apps that instantly remove eyebags, whiten teeth and 'improve' skin tone, and in ever more advertising from cosmetics companies, the skincare industry, dentists and cosmetic surgeons. Every young woman in this research reported seeing *multiple communications every day* telling them that they should work harder, buy more expensive products or undergo treatments or cosmetic procedures in order to look and feel better.

In this chapter I look at what young women said about 'the beauty industry on my phone' and at how social media are reshaping their ideas of what is 'normal' or 'attractive', 'unacceptable' or 'wrong'. I locate my discussion in the context of trends that make up the assemblage of 'neoliberal beauty' with its emphasis upon working on, monitoring and optimizing the self to be 'the best you can be'. I also situate the discussion in the context of the pandemic, which saw a decrease in posting to social media but a significant increase in beauty content. Much has been written about pro-ana, fitspo, influencers, makeovers; here I turn my attention to a less well-researched aspect of the beauty industry: smartphone apps. I show how these apps are contributing to the creation of a 'pedagogy of defect'[1] through which young women come to see their own faces and bodies as not good enough, as failing, and document the ways the apps make connections to cosmetic surgery and other procedures (e.g. fillers and injectables), aiding in the mainstreaming of these interventions. I show how through these apps young women are encouraged to scan and surveil themselves for problems and flaws, which may not even be visible to the naked eye. And I demonstrate the emergence of new forensic and metricized ways of looking at the self and others.

Everywhere and all the time: contemporary beauty pressures

The communications about appearance that young women engage with on their socials are the product of multiple and contradictory trends: the increasing entanglement of the beauty industry with surgical, pharmaceutical and genetics industries; a growing overlap between beauty and 'wellness', including 'clean eating', 'fitspiration' ('fitspo') and positive health discourses; an emphasis on a positive 'mindset' and on beauty as a 'state of mind'; the diversification of mainstream beauty ideals to include bigger, older and disabled models as well as more women of colour, queer and nonbinary models; and the emphatic focus on the 'perfectibility' of the body, and on the compulsory nature of beauty work. These trends operate within a digital culture that foregrounds bodies – particularly women's bodies – as central to their personal worth or value. As feminist media scholar Alison Winch puts it: 'In the hyper-visible landscape of popular culture the body is recognized as the object of women's labour: it is her asset, her product, her brand and her gateway to freedom and empowerment.'[2]

Neoliberal beauty

Underpinning these trends is a neoliberal culture in which the requirement to be 'beautiful' is extending, intensifying and also moving inside.[3] The way that beauty pressures are extending can be seen in how the requirement to look good has extended to times or periods in a life that were previously considered outside a focus on appearance. The beauty industry has shifted deeper into childhood, as media, cosmetics and fashion companies have moved in on younger age groups with beauty-focused teen magazines and product ranges.[4] For example, Clarins' slogan is 'Beautiful at every age' and advertising and in-store branding includes the pull quote 'In beauty it is never too early and never too late.' Pregnancy, too, no longer represents an escape from or relaxation of the demands of beauty,[5] and, moreover, getting back to one's pre-baby weight is represented in popular media as women's crowning achievement, with predictable effects on increased fear and anxiety around appearance in the postpartum period.[6] Furthermore, appearance messages targeted to women going through menopause are one of the fastest growing areas of the beauty industry.

The extension of beauty pressures is also to be found in the expansion of areas of the body that have become the focus of attention and are seen to require work and products. 'Upper arm definition' became a major preoccupation in the late 1990s; armpits were a new target in the mid-2000s (see, for example, Dove's video 'An Open Letter to the Armpit'[7]). These campaigns were closely followed by more focus on the eyebrows (mentioned by almost everyone I interviewed), the suggestion of the 'thigh gap' as a standard of bodily desirability, alongside the invention of new constructs such as the 'bikini bridge', the 'underboob', the 'thigh brow', etc.

As well as spreading out, the beauty industrial complex is also intensifying dramatically. This is facilitated by a 'surveillant imaginary' that is 'expanding vertiginously'.[8] More than a decade ago, writing a book about *Gender and the Media*, I argued that 'surveillance of women's bodies . . . constitutes perhaps the largest type of media content across all genres and media forms'.[9] Today that is not only still true, but surveillance is operating at ever finer-grained levels, and becoming forensic in its gaze as I explore later in the chapter. It is striking that microscopes, telescopic gunsights, peep holes, callipers and set squares have become ubiquitous in beauty advertising. Images of cameras and of perfect 'photo beauty' and of 'HD-ready' skin also proliferate, along with several brands which incorporate 'Insta' in their name, e.g. InstaSkincare Retinol Serum. Most common of all are the motifs of the tape measure (often around the upper thigh) and the magnifying glass, used to scrutinize pores, sun damage or broken capillaries, but – more importantly at a meta level – underscoring the idea of women's appearance as under constant magnified surveillance.

One case in point is Benefit's POREfection campaign, which constructs facial beautification through an analogy with espionage, rendering women as 'spygals' checking skintone and the appearance of pores (blocked, too big, etc.). Perfumier Douglas also deploys a magnifying glass trope, repeatedly encouraging its consumers to forensically analyse what is wrong with a face (our own or others') and how it can be improved (e.g. is it too 'wide', 'thin', 'round', 'square', is the nose too 'broad' or too 'long'?). These are just a few examples attesting to the way in which an ever refined (and punitive) visual literacy of the female face is being normalized, and has intensified with the prevalence of high-definition digital photographic technologies. As I discuss in chapter 4, this connects vividly to young women's sense of being watched and judged constantly.

Thirdly, the beauty industry is also moving 'inside'. This can be seen in the proliferating number of products marketed to women to swallow/ingest that promote the 'beauty immune system', including standard formulations of multi-vitamins and minerals sold to women as beauty products – e.g. 'Perfectil'[10] – and daily drinks that promote collagen, antioxidant defences, etc. It is also seen in the ever more intense psychologization of appearance-related work, which involves changing your mindset to become attractive or, alternatively, to become more disciplined so that you work harder to make yourself attractive. This may be promoted via 'positive' mantras such as 'confidence is the new sexy',[11] 'where purchase of the product will produce confidence which then magically transforms into desirable appearance, or indeed via 'wellness messages'.[12] It may also be pushed through tougher disciplinary messages such as those that characterize fitspo: 'This month's choices are next month's body', 'Be stronger than your excuses', or 'You can have results or excuses. Not both'.[13]

It is in this distinctive contemporary context that young women engage with the ubiquitous beauty content on their phones. It is a cultural context in which the body is understood as an ongoing 'project' and in which looking your best has taken on the status of a moral imperative – the ugly, abject flipside of which is 'letting yourself go'. Young women understand themselves as being required to work on their appearance, as being responsible for changing and improving their bodies. They are active in spending time learning about different products, treatments and exercise regimes, as well as in self-tracking and self-monitoring in multiple ways[14] (e.g. counting steps, tracking exercise, enumerating calories, monitoring menstrual cycles and keeping records of corresponding data such as food cravings, weight gain or loss and skin breakouts). They work on their actual physical bodies, faces, hair, and they also invest time, money and labour in their digital images. In doing so, young women both uphold and resist the ubiquitous messages about work, consumption and self-optimization. They 'learn' from the beauty content they encounter, they sometimes 'feel inspired', or 'motivated', but also experience feelings of shame, despair and self-hatred.

The normalization of cosmetic surgery

This research underscores a growing body of evidence about the normalization of cosmetic surgery and cosmetic procedures including Botox, fillers and liposuction.[15] It further highlights the way these are increasingly targeted at younger women – the so-called 'Baby Botox' trend. The language used to describe these procedures is crucial to their growing acceptability, with words such as 'tweakments'[16] suggesting something minor and non-invasive, and phrases like 'preventative Botox' adding a sheen of moral value associated with foresight and planning. The mainstreaming of cosmetic procedures is also facilitated by the light touch regulation of such procedures, frequently carried out by those with minimal training, and promoted as something to get done in your 'lunch hour'.[17] Botox became available in high street store Superdrug in 2018, and in 2022 more than one million Botox injections were given in the UK.[18] In the late 2010s surgeons reported that women would often bring pictures of celebrities or influencers with them to demonstrate the look they hoped to achieve,[19] highlight-ing the entanglement of media and celebrity culture in the normalization of cosmetic surgery.[20] Increasingly, today, would-be patients bring digitally enhanced images of *themselves*,[21] and ask surgeons to recreate the effects that were achieved via photo editing on their digital image – a topic that requires much more research.

Women in their late teens and early twenties told me they were seeing multiple promotions for cosmetic procedures every time they were online. 'All. The. Time', said one interviewee, emphatically, when I asked her if she ever saw adverts for treatments and surgeries. Lynne, 19, reported: 'Definitely. Lip fillers I get. *Loads* of skin treatment ones. Sometimes bum enhancers'. For Anna, a white 21-year-old who was furloughed from her job in a restaurant, it was mostly cosmetic dental treatments: 'teeth straightening, teeth whitening, really all the time, Invisalign stuff'.[22] She explained this as a consequence of having watched lots of 'before and after' videos, which she – like many – found really interesting. Lily also enjoyed watching makeover videos and described the feeling of satisfaction she gets from 'seeing nose jobs, lip fillers, people getting their teeth done'. As she put it, 'it's kind of nice to see that people have had it done, like it's satisfying to see how much of a difference it has made to someone's face'. But while individual transformations might feel inspiring, the cumulative effect was overwhelming:

> It's been coming up on my page . . . I get quite a lot on my Instagram . . . get bigger lips, get more cheekbones in here, and an eyebrow lift. And the fact that I even know about this, it's just *bad*. And you just feel like . . . You see all these people getting it, getting that look. And it's like, what is this, what is it supposed to be, like that standard of perfection. So then you look down on yourself, and it's just . . . It's just like a spiral down from there. (Lily, 20)

Lily's comments highlight the ambivalence about appearance-related content among many young women, their sense of being both attracted and repelled; the way that enthusiasm co-existed with criticism and distress, with 'spiralling down' and 'looking down on yourself'.

It was striking to note the difference in attitude between older and younger participants, which reinforced the sense – reported by many – that appearance pressures are 'getting worse' (Soraya, 20). Sofia, 25, said that: 'I'm an old person on TikTok. I'm like the grandma of TikTok (laughter).' This advanced age allowed her to highlight numerous contrasts between her own generation and what she saw as the platform's typical demographic, particularly in relation to the mainstreaming of cosmetic procedures of all kinds. 'Plastic surgery's becoming normalized', she told me. For her age group she believed it would have been 'taboo' or 'hush hush' to talk about 'getting work done' but for younger TikTokers:

> They all come forward with all their plastic surgeries being, like, 'this is what you need to ask for, I got it done here' . . . They all get their lips done. They all get nose jobs. They all get their eyes lifted to like like . . . there's that model look where they want their eyes to look like a cat. Like a tiger. I'm like 'woah'! Loads of stuff like that. And Botox. Girls get Botox now and they call it preventative Botox.

Although only two years younger, Bipasha, 23, exemplified this shift. Styling herself as a fan of the TOWIE[23] lifestyle, she told me:

> If people are getting a little bit of lip filler to make themselves look better, I don't think there's anything wrong with that. I think when it goes overboard, then I think then there's obviously something wrong with the person . . . I think there is a limit. I don't agree with people completely transforming their faces and trying to get something done and getting it done cheap and then ruining their faces with it and getting ill and

infections and stuff like that . . . but with lip fillers and that it's
not a big deal . . . A bit of Botox, a little bit of getting your lips
done . . . it's part of our generation. It's normal.

She remarked that she would feel 'very pressured' to get a 'lip
job' if she didn't have full lips, and wouldn't hesitate to get it
done. But she added quickly 'My mum would murder me.'

Alba, at just 20, also felt the pressure to consider surgical
or other cosmetic procedures. She told me 'quite a few of my
friends have had their lips done' and that it was important to
her 'not to judge'. 'It's the pressure we are under', she explained.
'It is coming in younger and younger.'

Pandemic paradoxes: aesthetic rest and investment

The pandemic exerted ambivalent and contradictory
impacts on many aspects of life, including social media and
experiences of its 'perfect' aesthetics. As discussed in the
Introduction, Covid created existential threats that were
experienced unevenly across the UK population, globally and
also among research participants. One interview participant
had become a carer during the pandemic; another participant
was working as a newly qualified doctor on an emergency
ward; a third experienced a major depressive mental health
crisis when she was dismissed from her job at the start of
the lockdown, and then experienced the breakdown of her
relationship with her boyfriend. During the course of the
research, several participants contracted Covid. By the end
of the interviewing period in June 2022 most had been ill, had
siblings or family members who had also been ill, and knew
many people who had developed long Covid. Several, tragi-
cally, had lost someone in their family or friendship circle,
in one case their mother who was in her fifties, in another a
27-year-old friend.

Against this context – matters of life and death; concerns about education, (un)employment, housing and money; and significant health and mental health issues – it might be assumed that discussions about social media, and particularly about appearance and self-presentation, would be seen as trivial or unimportant. This was categorically not the case. Young people were going out less and they were posting less, but they were no less engaged in deliberating about how they wanted to use their social media, how they wanted to present themselves, who they wanted to 'be'. Indeed, if anything, the pandemic had given some young people both a reason and an opportunity to 'press pause' (as one participant put it) and re-evaluate several aspects of their lives and their relationships. As discussed in chapter 1, many told me that they had undertaken some 'cleansing' of their social media, aiming to make it reflect their current interests and priorities, in some cases 'purging' accounts they had previously followed. The language of cleanliness was striking in the context of public health messages centred on hand-washing and the use of disinfectants.

The impact of the pandemic on pressures to live up to 'perfect' images was paradoxical. In some senses the tyranny of the perfect loosened its grip. As I discuss in chapter 5, many experienced the pressure to post regularly as less intense. Many participants stayed at home most of the time, and there was much humour among my interviewees (as well as across the rest of the population) about what many described as 'basically living in pyjamas, trackies and sweatpants'. Alongside 'cleansing' their social media, many young women seemed to practise a form of *aesthetic resting*, yet they were also simultaneously *investing* in their appearance, capitalizing the self, and were involved in diverse projects of *self-discipline and self-optimization*. They also reported spending considerably longer than usual watching beauty-related content on social media.

Simidele Dosekun coined the phrase 'aesthetic vigilance' to capture the way that participants in her study of practices of femininity in Lagos, Nigeria, took time out or gave their bodies a break from the beauty practices in which they were routinely involved. She argues that 'with the postfeminist intensification of feminine beauty norms and the attendant, commodified proliferation of beauty technologies or "solutions", the pursuit of beauty comes to pose heightened, embodied and psychic risks for women'. In this context, 'aesthetic vigilance' is a means of 'risk-managing one's attachments to beauty and its technologies'.[24] Like Dosekun's participants, my interviewees frequently discussed various forms of 'aesthetic rest' they were undertaking during lockdown. Common among these were taking out weaves or hair extensions, removing nail extensions or gel/acrylic nails, and taking a break from the use of semi-permanent makeup and from wearing false eyelashes. One particularly vivid example was the decision of Anna, 21, to shave off her long hair after she found out that she was being furloughed from her job in a restaurant. It might be tempting to read this as some kind of expression of anger or protest, but Anna took care to explain to me that it was actually a unique opportunity to allow her hair the chance to heal and grow back anew, after nearly a decade in which she had been bleaching it and it had become dry, coarse and broken. Other participants used very similar language to describe their own breaks from various beauty practices – removal of varnish gave nails chance to 'breathe', cutting down on hair dye, hair straightening or extensions was also 'good for my hair', and so on.

However, this kind of rest from particular beauty practices was not – or at least not only – an end in itself but also a means of *investing in* one's appearance for the longer term. That is, it was a form of what Julia Coffey calls 'body work'[25] – the ways people work on their bodies to align with socio-cultural ideals. Young women hoped that their commitment to taking a break would reap rewards in terms of having stronger hair, better skin, healthier nails, etc. Many went further than this in using the opportunity of the pandemic to deliberately try to *add value* to their appearance. Ches persuaded her parents to pay for invisible braces to straighten her teeth, arguing that the lockdown (which for her meant time away from university) would give her the opportunity to stay at home (and therefore not to be seen) for many weeks, and also the time needed to focus on the dental care required – an onerous task involving taking out the braces before every meal and thoroughly cleaning them and her teeth before re-inserting them. She also explained that she used lockdown to buy an expensive eyelash serum that would, she hoped, give her longer and thicker lashes by the end of the pandemic. In Ches's case, as with other participants who invested in skin care products, hair masks, etc., there was a thoughtful attempt to use the time of lockdown to optimize and add value to one's looks.

In addition to cleansing, resting and investing, participants also undertook various exercise and self-transformation projects. In the UK, the most prominent national challenge by some way was 'PE with Joe Wicks' which exhorted the entire population to 'get fit' during lockdown with his daily exercise programme screened on the BBC. 'Couch to 5K' also remains hugely popular, as do skipping, yoga and cycling challenges. YouTube is a key site of fitness and beauty challenges, and many of my participants also commented on the proliferation of such challenges on TikTok – relating to skincare, haircare, self-care, mental health and fitness of every kind. Interviewees enjoyed these challenges, often being spurred on by motivational content promising 'we are going to come out of this isolation with the most amazing body ever, the most amazing face ever, the best mental health ever'. They were also amused by videos in which an 'ordinary person' with a 'regular' (i.e. not normatively perfect) body undertakes an 'influencer regime' for a limited period of time. The specificity of some of the challenges undertaken by young women was striking: Nadine was undertaking a hair mask challenge, which she said involved her fermenting bowls of rice around her home in an effort to create a mask that would make her hair thicker and healthier; and Lily was doing various 'side jaw' challenges, to tone flesh under her chin. She commented on her deep ambivalence about the endeavour. It was making some kind of a difference, she said, but:

> it's like you start to look at yourself and you notice things you didn't before ... So there's been like a side profile trend. And you see all these people with really good side profiles. And you see a nice jawline and whatnot. And you know, I'd never thought before, oh I look bad from the side ... But then I started taking pictures of myself from the side as well. And you know when you see your own jawline or side profile you're like, well why does mine look like that. And it's kind of upsetting ... And then you read the comments ... And it just puts you down a little bit.

Social media pedagogies

Lily's account is a vivid illustration of what Susan Bordo, writing more than thirty years ago, called a 'pedagogy of defect' – namely the way that young women are incited to see and come to know themselves through a focus on defects – on what is wrong, faulty and how they could improve their appearance. The term pedagogy captures a combination of teaching and learning and it also directs attention to different styles of sharing knowledge – for example the difference between learning by rote and learning through experience. The term has recently come to prominence in analyses of digital culture. Sometimes this is explicit, as can be seen in Kim Toffoletti and Holly Thorpe's analysis of the #Bikini Body Guide, which they argue draws on a range of affectively or emotionally loaded ways of communicating in order to promote the programme.[26] These include the promotion of feelings of pride in the exercising body; community recognition of hard work; relatability and authenticity, including expressions of vulnerability; and contrasts between shame and achievement in the before and after body. Natalie Hendry, Catherine Hartung and Rosie Welch talk about 'influencer pedagogy' to discuss how influencers cultivate authenticity and expertise to educate their followers.[27] More broadly, as Wright has argued, a postfeminist pedagogy instructs and regulates girls and young women's subjectivities.[28] This occurs, Kylie Jarrett reminds us, through the organization of platforms so that 'the correct training of individuals occurs'.[29] As Rich and Miah have argued, much social media content has an 'absence of explicit learning goals' but nevertheless is designed to teach particular attitudes and ways of being.[30] Maria-José Camacho-Miñano and colleagues describe as 'biopedagogies' the ways in which young women come to learn about bodies and appearance via digital spaces like Instagram, via a range of different content that communicates what the perfect you should look like.[31]

In the remainder of this chapter, I will look at how the notion of a pedagogy of defect has even more power and relevance today than when Bordo was writing (pre social media and smartphones). Most research to date has examined pedagogies in relation to influencer, peer and health/beauty content on social media. Here I will focus, by contrast, on smartphone beauty apps. I will show how they deliberately and ever more minutely break down the face and body into problem zones that can then be addressed by the cosmetics, skincare and surgery companies that comprise the beauty industrial complex. I will demonstrate that in the process they are creating new visual literacies that are quite different than anything that has gone before, and inculcating new forensic ways of seeing and evaluating that young women apply to themselves and to others.

Beauty apps

Beauty apps are smartphone applications that subject the face and body to intense forms of surveillance that offer fine-grained, forensic and metric scrutiny with the stated goal of improving a selfie, teaching cosmetic techniques, identifying problems, rating an image or trying out potential changes, from new hair colour to a reshaped nose. The apps of course do many other things – including building a library of facial recognition images, and harvesting vast amounts of data from the people who use them – a topic that requires much more critical research. Jill Walker Rettberg asks us to raise critical questions about such technologies, which are passing so seemingly smoothly into everyday life for so many people – including participants in this research. 'What is filtered out?' she asks, and 'what are the consequences of seeing ourselves as data bodies?'[32] It is clear that racial biases are built into many of these apps; they represent what Ruha Benjamin brilliantly dissects as the New Jim Code: 'the employment of new technologies that reflect and reproduce existing inequities but that are promoted and perceived as more objective or progressive than the discriminatory systems of a previous era'.[33] One example is the emphasis upon skin 'brightening' or 'lightening' in these apps, which encodes particular ideas about skin colour and desirability that have been built into photography itself, in which film exposures were designed for Caucasian skin. This is 'engineered inequity', Benjamin argues. What counts as beautiful is also built into 'algorithms of oppression'[34] centred on the privileging of whiteness and on the denigration of people of colour – something experienced as a felt reality by many of my interviewees, as we saw in chapter 2.[35]

There are many different types of apps and a Google search on the term 'beauty apps' in December 2022 generated more than 3 *billion results*. Perhaps the best-known appearance-related app type is the photo-editing or selfie-modification app, such as Facetune or BeautyCam, with versions of such technologies now present in smartphone hardware and within social media platforms/applications such as Instagram and Snapchat. Facetune promises to help users achieve 'perfect smiles' by widening your smile or whitening your teeth; to give you 'beautiful skin' by smoothing, brightening and removing any imperfections; to emphasize your eyes, giving you a 'penetrating gaze' or changing eye colour or shape; to 'reshape facial structure' including nose, jaw, cheekbones; to apply makeup including blush, eye shadow, lipstick; and to enhance photos in myriad other ways. It is interesting to note that in their latest advert for the app, which uses AI, the developer Lightricks employs a vocabulary and iconography of individualism, confidence and defiance that has become widespread in commercial messages directed to women[36]: enjoining potential users to 'Highlight what makes you, you' and 'Let your visual content shine'. A banner horizontally scrolling across the screen declares: 'Dream it* Describe it* Create It*'. Young women used these apps routinely, almost never posting without editing pictures in some way. Indeed, Nazanin, 18, said that the *platforms themselves* give the impression that the real unfiltered 'you' was not good enough:

> The thing is, for instance, the actual social media platform almost encourages that behaviour. On Snapchat, you have all of these different filters of like better lighting or that make your face look slimmer. And if it's there . . . If it wasn't there, then people wouldn't be using it.
>
> And on Instagram, when you come to post something, there are all those different kinds of filters and stuff that you can change before you click post. It's almost like the platform is encouraging you to change you for them. And I don't remember the last time that someone was, oh, just going to post . . . Just take a picture of myself as I am now and post that. It just doesn't, it just rarely, rarely happens.

A second type of app that young women said they used is the 'personal tutelage' app, which offers instruction in techniques to enhance appearance. This might include teaching the makeup technique of contouring, eyebrow shaping or learning about which colours work together. Dubbing themselves as 'your own personal stylist on your phone' such apps work towards customizable solutions such as 'instant, personalized nail polish and makeup suggestions to suit your mood and complete your look' (L'Oreal Colour Genius). There are some overlaps between these and a third type of 'try out' apps which offer the opportunity to try out different looks ranging from a new hair style or colour, new makeup, teeth whitening through to major surgical interventions such as nose reconstruction, breast augmentation or vulval surgery. On submission of a selfie, the apps will help to 'visualize a new you' (FaceTouchUp). While some of the apps are marketed as 'fun' – e.g. see how you look with blue hair, or as a boy, or as an anime character – others position themselves as aiding in the decisions about surgery or other cosmetic procedures. FaceTouchUp promises: 'we bring you the same digital imaging technology that surgeons use to visualize plastic surgery results – all in a super easy to use site. For nose jobs, chin augmentation, liposuction, breast reshaping and more. FaceTouchUp is the virtual plastic surgery tool you've been waiting for'.[37] As noted elsewhere, 'horizontal links with the plastic surgery industry are well-established – indeed surgeons ply their services on this kind of site or app' and are told that the app will 'attract new patients, elevate your practice and increase patient acceptance, satisfaction and word of mouth'.[38]

A different genre of app is the aesthetic benchmarking app which offers the ability to be 'rated' on questions such as 'How old do I look?', 'How attractive am I?' or 'Am I ugly?'. These apps invite users to benchmark aspects of their appearance and were widely used among my participants. Often young women told me that they submitted photos of themselves to such apps 'for a laugh' or 'when I'm bored'. For example, Alba, 20, told me she encountered the opportunity to get 'rated' (*in-app*) on Snapchat and Instagram:

> Oh yes, I only really use them if they come up on Snapchat or Instagram just if I'm bored. But yes I have done those. There's some on Instagram that rate your face as well. Which is probably completely random. But yes there's a few of those on Instagram.

For others, however, the endeavour had a more serious side to it. Ches, 20, told me that she had never liked her nose, and had submitted pictures of her face to several of these (machine vision) apps that give 'scores' and 'feedback' and she said she had her feelings about her nose 'confirmed' – which she found upsetting. She was careful not to create any drama around the experience, saying 'it wasn't like "oh shock, what's this like upstaying news"' it was more like '"yes, thought so"'. However, it also made her feel that 'unless I get a nose job I can't improve that score', further underscoring the relation between these apps and the mainstreaming of cosmetic surgery. For the time being, it convinced her to decide 'well I won't get pictures from that side' and alerted her to 'know my angles' (a common observation among young women).

For Ches, as for many young women, it was very hard to come to a realistic appraisal of their appearance: they worried that their parents would be biased towards seeing them as attractive, and friends might be flattering (at least to their face) with what Handyside and Ringrose call inspo paras (inspirational paragraphs),[39] messages of support and ego-boosts. The apps trade on precisely this concern, promoting themselves via messages that ask 'Do you ever wonder if you're ugly and your friends just don't tell you?'. By contrast they present their own authority as rooted in scientific judgement. This is the 'ideology of dataism',[40] a central part of 'metric culture'.[41] 'Test yourself!' Facemeter exhorts. Another app explains, 'when your friends won't tell you, the Ugly Meter will'. As with the try-out apps, there are powerful links with the cosmetic and surgical industries, including direct exhortations to 'improve your score' by undergoing hyaluronic acid treatment/laser hair removal/a chemical peel, etc.

Scanning apps and the metric gaze

The final type of app discussed here combines elements of the others; it is the self-surveillance app, which promises to scan and scrutinize the face and body for flaws, damage and problems that may not even be visible to the naked eye. At the medical end of the spectrum there are apps which will allow you to use your phone like a scanner to identify potential problems: maybe you have freckles or moles that are changing shape which may signal the development of a skin cancer; perhaps you are developing broken capillaries or even varicose veins. Apps like UMSkinCheck and SofferVein can help 'diagnose' such problems. Sunburn, smoking damage and dental problems can also be assessed using this kind of app (e.g. CoppertoneMyUV alert; Dental X-Ray; Smoking Time Machine). They may contain useful features, e.g. setting a timer for sunbathing/applying sunscreen, alerting a visit to a medical professional if a mole has changed shape.

Far more numerous are the cosmetics/skincare industry apps that promise a full report on your skin or face on submission of a selfie and some basic information. Almost all the big players in the industry have moved into this field, including brands like L'Oreal, Clinique, Neutrogena, Nivea, Olay and Vichy. Replacing a traditional beauty salon visit, the apps promise to deliver detailed analysis and a 'prescription' of products tailored precisely to 'you'. The language used emphasizes the authority, expertise and use of 'breakthrough technology'. Clinique's Clinical Reality is claimed to be based on more than 50 years of dermatological research enhanced by 'more than one million face scans'. Biotherm's app Skin Diag 'combines the latest AI technology with Biotherm's scientific research'. Alongside the precision of results is an emphasis upon the ease and rapidity of using such apps which takes just 'seconds'.

Images on the apps or their website equivalents use familiar sci-fi-style imagery which shows a woman's face being subjected to 'analysis' as she holds her phone up. Beams of light, grids and matrices superimposed upon the face underscore the idea of this as a future technology that is available right now. In their discussion of these apps, and Lame Kenalemang and Göran Eriksson highlight the 'scientifization of beauty' reinforced by the use of biological terms and an iconography from the laboratory (lab coats, white gloves, etc.). The 'results' also add to this scientific authority and are presented in diagrams, tables and charts, with written reports about problem areas, immediately followed by advice on how to improve:

> Here are some tips for preserving your skin's youthful appearance . . . Preventing wrinkles requires acting on the thickness of the epidermis by stimulating its natural renewal and acting on the dermis by promoting the synthesis of its compounds. Pure Retinol has this capacity, use it at night with an SPF the next morning to protect your skin. (Skin Genius, L'Oreal[42])

As well as using facial recognition and scanning software to lend authority to the production of what are essentially, then, personalized advertisements for products like Retinol or collagen, these apps also operate more broadly to intensify the forensic gaze on women's faces. Indeed, they go further in converting it into multiple data points which correspond to areas of the face and their associated 'problems'. This offers an augmented metric gaze on the face, inciting women to consider

their faces in extraordinary detail and specificity. Neutrogena's
Skin360, for example, offers 90 different possible scores from
its scan of the face. It is as if the scan 'could perform an almost
microscopic examination'.[43] This dramatically intensifies the
'pedagogy of defect' discussed earlier, and calls forth a subject
who knows and monitors herself forensically. This is producing new ways of seeing: forms of looking and evaluating that
are specific, forensic, judgemental and are practised by women
on each other and on themselves.

New ways of seeing

It is clear that new visual literacies – particularly of the face
– are being quite deliberately trained and inculcated by the
beauty industry, which has an interest in women knowing and
seeing themselves through a lens of fear and dissatisfaction. It
is also becoming clear that younger women's ways of seeing are
quite different, and far more forensic, than those undertaken
by older generations, as they have been 'trained' to look, to
magnify, to evaluate in ways that are historically new. Indeed,
this was something that was noted as a difference even among
my 18–28-year-old cohort, with younger women having a
very highly developed visual literacy of the face in particular.
Sofia, who had introduced herself to me as 'like the grandma of
TikTok' at 25 years old, told me that these new visual literacies
have developed during her lifetime:

> It's crazy, I think. The specificity. I feel like when I was young
> it was just like, oh, thin or fat, or pretty not pretty. There was
> obviously certain things, like everyone wanted to have a nice
> bum, but not with this degree of observation and obsession
> on specific, tiny little features. How should your eyebrows be?
> How should your right tooth, left molar look? It's crazy. Crazy
> amounts of specificity.

I spoke to several of my female participants about this impression, after they frequently highlighted what they saw as major flaws in their own faces or bodies, despite all appearing to me to be attractive young women. Often I had the experience of literally *not being able to see* the flaw to which they were referring. This is not about poor eyesight on my part but about the cultural lens I brought to the practice of looking. I have written about this in relation to my students, noting that my own way of seeing feels both less intense and more benign:

> When I hear younger women talking in detail about contouring, or brow definition or about different mascara effects – upon only having seen an image of a face for a fraction of a second – my own 'glance' is revealed to me as something like a blur, so little information does it offer. It is as if newer visual literacies generate high definition digital pictures, while my own rendered image is a low resolution one, which generates an overall impression but none of the specificity.[44]

Eve laughed at my failure to see the details of a photographed face, saying that I was like her mum: 'My mum's the same. Yes definitely. When my mum looks at a photo she'll just think oh Eve's smiling in that, that's nice, she wouldn't assess the small details.' By contrast, Eve said that she can apprehend *multiple* aspects of a photograph of a face within the briefest of moments, including being able to tell 'instantly' whether it has been edited or not or filtered or augmented in any way. This shows forcefully that young women actually see differently and more forensically. They practise what Ana Elias and I have called 'nanosurveillance' and a 'metric gaze', and Lavrence and Cambre dub a 'digital forensic gaze'.[45] As Soraya expressed it: 'I think people really do consider every little thing about a photo'.

In a recognition of how these forensic judgemental gazes do not arise spontaneously but are actively tutored or learned,

Lily reflected on how, since her immersion in TikTok's side jaw trends during lockdown, she has herself become a reluctant evaluator of her friends' faces – assessing them for how toned they are, how they look from different angles, something she said she would never have even thought about before:

> Yes. So now that I'm around my friends, I always look at their side profiles now to see if they've got a nice jawline. Which is just really bad, I never actually used to do it before, never paid attention to it at all.

Lily said this with candour – she was extremely honest and reflective about all these processes. She also said it with sadness. Like Elizabeth, the 23-year-old junior doctor we met in the Introduction banging the side of her head to try to dislodge the toxic ideas that had taken residence in there, Lily deeply regretted this new way of seeing and judging. It was not something she felt she had chosen.

Conclusion: the costs of the perfect

In this chapter I have documented further what young women told me was a requirement to appear 'perfect' at all times on social media. They highlighted the exacting appearance ideals they feel they have to try to live up to, which come from celebrities, influencers, peers, the platforms themselves and from the beauty industrial complex. These are experienced by young women as ever more fine-grained and punitive: not 'just' a slim but curvy body, perfect skin and hair, and straight white teeth, but so much more: carefully groomed eyebrows; long, curled eyelashes; large, full lips; hollows at the hips; a tight 'side jaw', etc. The list is seemingly endless and ever-expanding, as the beauty industry colonizes ever more areas creating new 'problems' requiring product solutions.

The chapter explored the paradoxical impact that the pandemic has had on the beauty pressures that young women experience – at once offering some respite, yet at the same time promoting the 'break' from normal life as an opportunity to invest in the body and appearance, through exercise, skin and hair care, cosmetic dentistry regimes and also through strategic aesthetic 'rest' and re-capitalization. Young women reported posting less but engaging with beauty content more during the pandemic, through challenges, makeover videos, tutorials and apps. Looking at the latter, I showed how smartphone apps contribute to the mainstreaming of cosmetic surgery. I also demonstrated that their focus on appearance is helping to bring into being ever more metricized and forensic ways of apprehending the body and face, and I suggested, echoing some participants, that these are materially affecting young women's ways of seeing.

In the next chapter I shift the focus from looking and seeing to being watched, highlighting the extent to which young women are enmeshed in relations of surveillance, judgement and harassment from which it is difficult to escape.

4

Being watched, judged and harassed

I feel very conscious of being watched . . . I don't want to be looked at in that way. (Helena, 28)

The previous chapter concluded with a discussion of the emergence of new forensic ways of seeing, influenced by the beauty industry's intensifying pedagogies of defect, the ubiquity of photo-editing software and hardware, and smartphone and platform affordances. I showed how the gaze that women turn on themselves is both forensic and critical; they do not just glance at photographs, they scrutinize them, looking for flaws and fails. In this chapter I turn the lens around to discuss their experiences of being watched. In doing so I add further depth and complexity to the sense young women conveyed of feeling subject to relentless critical evaluation and judgement.

Young women told me that they feel under almost constant scrutiny both on- and offline. They described being 'stared at' in public spaces including bars, transport and the streets, and often being afraid. They feel themselves to be listened to by their devices, and tracked and monitored by the apps they use. They are subjected to sexual harassment and other intimate intrusions so regularly that many dismissed the experiences as barely worthy of comment – just some 'creeps' and 'weirdos', they said. And their friendship groups do not necessarily provide sanctuary from these experiences, instead representing a 'girlfriend gaze'[1] that is both surveillant and forensic. All these experiences are in turn amplified by the wider context of a culture in which women's bodies are subject to constant negative scrutiny and evaluation. This research provides a vivid illustration of the way this broader hostile culture of surveillance of, and cruelty towards, women in public life has a silencing and disciplining effect on *all* women.[2]

To explore this further the chapter is divided into three main parts. In the first, I look at what young women said about feeling watched, and how this is shaped by broader hostile cultures centred on critical evaluations of women in public life, and the trolling and shaming of women. In the second part, I discuss women's multiple experiences of harassment, abuse and threats of violence on social media – from comments about their bodies, to unsolicited dickpics, to stalking. The third part considers being watched and looked at by friends and peers, picking up on a motif that is highlighted throughout this book, namely the complicated entanglement of practices of care and cruelty among young women.

Surveillance of women in public

All the eyes and all the hands

A pervasive sense of feeling under surveillance was evident across the interviews. Young women told me that they feel that they are watched and evaluated wherever they go, not only on social media but in public life more generally. This formed a key *context* for being looked at and judged on their socials, and the experience of surveillance (and indeed harassment) also *flowed across and between* social media platforms and other everyday settings such as schools, workplaces, bars and the streets. This kind of looking was practised particularly by men. Rosa, 21, a white woman who worked full time as a waitress, spoke at length about being stared at in her workplace. She talked about customers coming to consume her as much as the food, and at how angry she felt about what she described memorably as 'all the eyes and all the hands', including those of her boss. She talked passionately about how these experiences were also causing her to re-evaluate similar experiences at school when male teachers had flirted with her and touched her inappropriately from her early teens onwards.

Eve, also 21, a white working-class student from Liverpool, likewise had much to say about the connections between being watched, being judged and being harassed on and off social media. She described 'groups of lads' as particularly threatening, not only in the way that they 'stare' at her and other women, but also how the staring may tip over into making 'derogatory comments'. These 'lads', she revealed, were not necessarily strangers but could be her friends, and might even include her boyfriend:

> I think there's always that lad culture when there's a big group of boys. I think if say one of them did say a derogatory comment about a woman I don't think any of the others would necessarily say anything, not through fear, but they'd be bothered that they'd get some sort of backlash in their social circle for speaking up.

She also described how groups of boys she knows well might cruelly dissect social media posts for fun and as a way of bonding as a group.[3] She said that they would see other forms of 'out there' sexism, such as wolf-whistling, as problematic, but would not see the link between those practices and their own behaviour.

> They wouldn't be the ones to whistle out of a car for example, they wouldn't be to that extent to women's faces. But I think

behind women's backs they'd make derogatory comments, talk about their bodies. I've seen them go on Tinder and have been like, oh she's ugly, but in a big group of them.

So it's not very nice, because that girl's obviously being commented on by a big group of boys, but I don't think they see the issue of that. It's just the extreme that they see the issue with, it's not the underlying issues that are less prevalent, less obvious I guess. (Eve, 21)

Eve's insights resonate with research by Laura Thompson[4] about some heterosexual men's abusive behaviour on dating apps.[5] She examines the Instagram sites Bye Felipe and Tinder Nightmares in which (mostly) women post about their experiences of receiving abuse on dating apps – usually when they do not respond quickly enough or enthusiastically enough to men's messages. The viciousness of the messages received is horrifying, and frequently includes racist abuse, fat-shaming and cruel assessments of the woman's appearance. Thompson's research analyses this in relation to individual hateful messages, but, as Eve's experience shows, it can also be a means of homosocial bonding among men, getting together variously to leer over or cruelly dissect women's bodies.

Several participants shared painful stories of precisely this kind of experience of harassment both in-person and online. One woman left a long, distressing comment on the survey to explain how she had routinely been made fearful by comments shouted at her by men in public space – from car windows or as she passed them in the street – but how a medication that caused her to gain weight had changed lascivious leering into brutal comments about her weight and undesirability. Lily, too, talked about her experience of boys being there to put you down. 'There are these hateful boys that try to bring you down', she said.

Helena, 28, a teacher, also talked about being stared at, locating it as part of a heteronormative visual economy as well as a gendered one.

I feel under surveillance everywhere. I've always felt surveilled – is that a word? – as a woman just even walking around
London or anywhere . . . That's one of the reasons I didn't get
social media, and why I definitely don't post pictures of myself.
That was a very active choice of mine and I make conscious
decisions on how I present myself to make sure that doesn't
happen.

Helena explained that she feels very uncomfortable with the
way she is observed and scrutinized while going about her
daily life. It is not just a male gaze, she explained, it is also a
heterosexual gaze, and as a lesbian woman, 'I'm completely
uninterested'. She described how she has struggled throughout
her life to avoid this unwanted form of being looked at, concluding that to actively defend against being stared at in this
way, she presents herself in a very particular manner:

I never wear makeup, oh actually I never wear makeup mostly
out of laziness, but there's also that dimension to it. I don't
really wear revealing clothes very often, if at all, and when I
do I feel very conscious of being watched. And so I generally
look like a bit of a slob when I go out unless I go to work . . .
And even if I were to go out for a drink or something I'd generally wear something not particularly revealing, and that is I
think definitely related to both my body image but also being
watched . . . I don't want to be looked at in that way.

For Praveena, 20, a student who wears a hijab in public, feeling watched was also a profoundly racialized experience, one
rooted in her religious identification as well as her gender and
brown skin. She talked of being stared at a great deal in public
places, such as on public transport:

Being a hijabi is already quite hard as we become a visible
representation of Islam so when people stare my first thought

is 'why are they staring at me?' and when the stare is longer than necessary, I start to wonder what they may have seen in the media and what they think about me and Islam overall. I never think it's about them being curious of the hijab . . . Being stared at definitely makes me feel very uncomfortable.

Camera culture

A different experience of being watched came from the taken-for-granted camera culture that was a feature of nights out as people generated content for their social media accounts. Lisa, 20, a white student, was one of several people who said she 'hated' being photographed:

Sometimes I go out with friends and they're posting. You get home and you watch the whole night back on Instagram because it's like having a TV crew with you.

She explained how this sense of being under constant surveillance made her feel she couldn't ever relax. Other people made similar remarks, sharing that they would be walking to the toilet in a nightclub, pulling their tummy in and wondering whose Instagram or Snapchat story they would end up on:

And also, it's a bit stressful because if you go out or whatever, you have to think. Because everyone's recording everything, you have to think . . . You can't let your guard down as much because you could see it again on someone's Snapchat or whatever. So you don't want to do anything embarrassing or [unclear] I'm thinking of on a night out, you definitely see people, women looking really worried about how they look, and it's two a.m. and no-one looks so nice. Because people are always taking photos, you can't really let your guard down. (Emma, 20)

Letitia, 27, a Black woman, furloughed from her job in retail, also said she felt very uncomfortable being photographed unless she was feeling unusually happy and confident:

> I'm not the most camera confident. So, usually, if I'm out, I see a camera, I'll usually run! (laughter) It's down to how happy I feel. But usually I'm not most confident when it comes to photos and such.

Holly, who took a lot of photographs and videos for her branded content (see chapter 5), experienced being stared at when she was the subject of photographs being taken by her mum, her friend or her boyfriend. Like Praveena, she was emphatic in explaining to me that this was not just people looking or being curious, it was a particularly hostile form of '*staring*':

> I hear people say oh, what is she doing? And it's really funny, because when you go out and you're taking photos, people just *stare*. I don't know why. Some people just walk past, but then other people literally stare at you like you're doing something you shouldn't be doing.

Besides a generalized sense of not being able to 'let your guard down' even on a night out with friends, or the discomfort of being stared at, a further fear was of ending up on a troll site. These are sites that traffic in photographs, or usually videos, of people taken without their consent (and often without their awareness). As Letitia explained:

> There are a lot of these troll pages on Instagram, and they pass themselves off as funny meme pages. But you look at a lot of their content, and it is bashing normal people. Or there will be a photo of someone doing something silly that maybe they shouldn't necessarily be doing. But it's like, at the end of the

day, I just don't think it's nice to feed into that, and it is quite toxic, I think.

Women are often pilloried on troll sites, frequently attacked for not being hot enough, being too fat, or, as I discuss in chapter 6, for being a 'slut' or a 'sket'. Even so-called #kindness videos can become exercises in humiliation for some people, while driving traffic to particular sites, at someone else's expense and without their consent.[6]

Cultures of cruelty

Troll sites are arguably just one example of a much wider pattern of cruelty and hostility directed at women in public life. This has been examined by decades of media scholarship documenting vicious evaluations of female politicians, celebrities, pop stars and others for falling short of 'perfect' physical appearance. Mainstream and legacy media have played a key part in this, with coverage in which no 'flaw' is too trivial to be picked over and magnified – and circled in red in the genre of celebrity and entertainment magazines, shows or digital content: the stretch mark, the cellulite dimple, the undepilated hair, the unflattering outfit. It is impossible to understand the heightened surveillance of women's bodies in contemporary culture without reference to celebrity culture with its circulating news articles, magazines, gossip sites and social media. Over the last decade we have also seen the dissemination and uptake of practices previously associated with the paparazzi such as 'the upskirt' shot or the use of other covert filming techniques, e.g. the scandal over the filming, then distribution via troll sites, of images of women eating whilst on train journeys or while working out in the gym. Central to all of this is the punitive regulation of women's bodies.

Many participants in this research found the hostile surveillance of female celebrities deeply upsetting, and they drew *direct* links between it and their own experiences. Letitia was one of several of my interviewees who had felt very upset by the hostile criticism that had greeted pop star Adele when she lost a significant amount of weight in 2020, seeing it as an example of completely unwarranted attacks on women in public life and as something that really 'got to me' personally. 'Leave her alone!' she implored:

> But, yes, or it could be someone's size. If someone's lost weight, or someone's gained weight, whatever. Like, recently . . . there was one page that was going mad over Adele and her weight loss, and there were all these theories of why she lost weight, or how she lost weight. And I thought, just leave her alone. It's not necessary. She's done it, and she's happy, then that's down to her.

Helena had a different take on the same story, but equally grounded in ideals of women's autonomy, and how troubling it is to see female celebrities' bodies up for constant public scrutiny and evaluation. Helena thought that Adele had been pressured by a sexist music industry to lose weight and to conform to normative appearance standards that she had been able to resist for so long. 'She's been got by the Americans', Helena said, and worried out loud whether another heroine of hers, Lizzo, would go that way too.

Lynne, in turn, talked about how affected she was by seeing British *Love Island* contestant Molly Mae attacked online. Explaining that the celebrity is the same age as her, she said that she and her sister felt moved to message Molly Mae as a small gesture of support in the midst of negative trolling that at one point caused Mae to take down her Instagram. (It should be noted that this was during Molly Mae's period as a contestant on the show, and pre-dates her much pilloried affirmations of neoliberal ideas about hard work and making it.)

Yes, I remember it was when they'd all come out of the villa and they did a reunion thing on ITV. And she was just getting . . . It was even the cast of *Love Island*. The other people who were on *Love Island* with her were just shouting at her and being like, oh, I haven't followed you because I don't like you and I think you're fake. And they were really probing her. And it made me feel so uncomfortable. It was the first time that I was like, oh, my gosh, *Love Island* probably is not good at all. Because these people, if they're already getting it from inside the crew, what are they going to get?

And I remember me and my sister both messaged her because we just like, she's probably never going to see this, but it would be nice, even, just a little message. Because I know she must get loads and loads of hate. And everyone was commenting 'Money May' on her thing. And all of her pictures saying she was just in it for the money. It was just awful. It was horrible . . . She's my age. She's one year older than me. I don't know how I would deal with that. I would have to delete Instagram. I would be distraught. So, yes. (Lynne, 19)

Looking at the comments that celebrities or influencers receive on their social media also had a chilling effect on many participants, and made them feel depressed, angry and fearful about 'all the hate' – as well as understandably anxious to avoid it themselves. Tanisha expressed it powerfully:

Tan: There's sexual comments, there's hateful comments, violent comments. And I'm sure that people who have a lot of followers don't even have time to look at all the comments, but just the fact that people can post things like that and it's there. So if a regular user like me is just scrolling through the comments I can see that . . . It's a lot. It's a lot (long exhale in distress)

RG: That is just so horrible. And what kind of effect does it have on you, just seeing that?

Tan: It makes me feel really scared, and angry ... I feel like
a lot of people wouldn't say those things in real life ... but
people feel really emboldened being behind the screen or
behind the keyboard.

Tanisha explained how seeing the comments that other
people receive – particularly other Black women – has had
a direct impact on her decision to keep her own Instagram
private:

I've gone back and forth in the past, whether or not I want to
make it public, but what stops me is ... anyone can follow you
... anybody can comment on your posts, and the things that
people say online is insane. I feel like, I like to think of myself
as a person who doesn't let a lot of things get to me, but I fully
acknowledge that I am a sensitive person, and I think that if I
was just, like, on social media to be critiqued like that, it would
not be good.

Intimate intrusions

Normalizing harassment

As well as being watched, stared at, photographed without their
consent and subjected to abusive comments, women were also
sexually harassed on a regular basis. Sexual harassment was not
something I planned to consider in this research, and the topic
was not included in the interview guide. But it was brought up
spontaneously in almost all the interviews as young women
told of regularly receiving lewd comments in response to
photos they have posted, as well as experiencing routine street
harassment. What was striking and especially disturbing was
how unremarkable – indeed almost expected – this seemed to
interviewees. As a rapid response review by the Government's
Department for Education[7] has confirmed, echoing feminist

research on sexual violence over decades, there is a 'shock-ing' normalization of sexual harassment and abuse in schools, colleges and wider society. Their official report found that 92 per cent of girls said that 'sexist name-calling happens a lot to them or their peers' and 'nearly 90% said they had been sent explicit pictures or videos of things they did not want to see' at least once, sometimes much more often. As this book was in the final stages of production in December 2022, Channel 4 screened an 'Undercover' documentary and commissioned a YouGov survey about sexual violence, which reinforced these figures: 71 per cent of women in the UK have experienced sexual harassment in a public place, one in four have been followed, and more than half of girls and young women said that they had been *sexually harassed while wearing their school uniform* (i.e. when they were under 16).[8]

When I asked if young women had ever received negative comments on their posts, they responded, as if as an after-thought: 'oh you get all the comments from men and stuff'. As Ruby, 27, put it: 'Some of it is just pervy men trying to flirt with you in a creepy way.' Mostly – young women explained – these were comments of a sexual nature, or were requests for nude selfies or unsolicited pictures of penises. Young women repeat-edly observed that these communications were from 'creeps' or 'weirdos' and 'you just block them'. The vast majority of the time they came from strangers, but they were more disturbing when they were sent by someone in their own network. Soraya, 20, said that someone she was at school with started sending her sexually harassing messages that made her so uncomfort-able that she eventually blocked him, only to have him create a new account to start messaging her:

And he was very forward with me and I was just really not happy with it and I just didn't like how weird he was being with me. And I told him quite a few times and it got to a point where he just wouldn't stop so I think I just blocked him and then I think a couple of years later he made a new account. Somehow he messaged me apologizing and saying something strange like, you were my dream or something really weird and I just blocked him again because I just found it really strange. But you know stuff like that I think happens to a lot of people, especially girls. Yes. But that was slightly different because he was at my school so he wasn't really a stranger but that was really weird.

Many of the young women I spoke with minimized the impact that such messages had on them, almost as if they were responding to an implicit expectation to be cool with all of this, and not to make a big deal of it. Holly told me jokingly about receiving multiple messages from 'just some random account on Instagram' that had been copied and pasted on many different photographs she had posted. These became more and more sexually graphic and also included a proposal of marriage. She told me: 'yes, you do get people like that saying funny things. But never any serious creepy stuff.' She concluded: 'I wouldn't say I've had any bad experiences at all.' It made me wonder how bad it would have to be to count as 'creepy stuff' or a 'bad experience'! Nevertheless, she went on to discuss the careful assessment she gives to message requests, trying to get information about the sender without/before opening them, and ignoring them if they seem to come from a random account, suggesting that she does indeed take these potential threats very seriously, even if there's a cultural demand operating not to seem bothered.

Safety work

As in Holly's case, it was notable how much thought and care young women put into managing their safety from potential harassers or 'creeps' online as well as offline. Although she also said creepy guys did not bother her much, Soraya said that this was the main reason she kept her Instagram private, and how she now checks up on people carefully before allowing them to follow her:

> So if I look at their account, I mean this is probably not the best thing to do, but I think is this person a normal person. If we've got mutual friends I don't even think twice, I let them follow me because if we've got mutual friends it's like Facebook. But if its someone who doesn't have any mutual friends and maybe their account doesn't look like a real account or it looks like they've got no followers or no pictures or something strange about them, I usually don't let them follow me.
>
> Because you can get weird creepy people messaging you or just weird. I've had all sorts of scenarios where random people have messaged me weird things, and been added to weird groups and then I've realized it might be because, I mean I've never wanted to make my profile public just because that idea scares me a bit. . . . I keep my account private . . . I think it's almost a way of me filtering who follows me.

Eve spoke about what she called a 'real dread' every time she opened Instagram, having previously linked it to her Tinder account. Even though, at the time of talking with me, she had been in a long-term relationship for over a year and no longer had a Tinder profile, she still got messages:

> And that's the bit where I dread opening because I'll probably have a message every couple of days, and it's always something either dodgy or weird . . . dick pics or men asking me to send them nudes, people I didn't even know. *I didn't ask for any of it, they just send it anyway . . . they're sending stuff that I don't want to be seeing.*

Eve had the very frightening experience of being stalked a few years earlier, when she was 17, by someone who knew where she went to school and eventually, after months of online harassment, turned up there as she was leaving to walk home one day. She reported it to a teacher who reported him to the police, but nothing happened (as so often in cases where women are stalked). Eve repeatedly blocked the man on Instagram, but every time she blocked one account, he would create another. Eventually he started using other social media, including Twitter, as she explained:

> Eve: And then I remember him tweeting, actually tweeting about me. It was a few years ago now, but I think he put 'Eve Castle I know you want to see me, don't pretend that you don't.' But obviously I was really embarrassed because everyone could see that, and he'd said my full name and things.
> RG: Oh Eve that's horrible.
> Eve: It got sorted eventually. I think he just realized that he was never going to get to me so he stopped making the Instagram accounts, but it wasn't a very nice experience.

These experiences led to Eve being understandably frightened about points of intersection between social media stalking and potential harassment and violence in her lived environment or neighbourhood. Other research highlights that cyber-stalking of women is a growing problem that is strongly connected to other digital crimes including misogyny and hate, doxing and identity theft. Most worryingly, it is also linked to escalations of physical violence against women.[9] Eve was one of a number of young women who noted the connection between the affordances of particular platforms and a feeling of never being safe:

> I think it's really scary that people can actually see your location on Snapchat. If you've got the maps turned on, that's a setting on it, then they can pinpoint exactly where you are when you're active on the app, which is scary in situations like that.

Similar concerns were raised in Laura Thompson's research about harassment on – and while using – dating apps. Her participants spoke of safety fears related to the geolocative features of such apps, in one case a woman describing coming within a few metres of someone she had met online, while simply putting out her garbage bins one evening.[10] Had he seen her he would immediately have known where she lived – information most dating app users keep secret in order to protect their safety unless or until they have built up trust. The Suzy Lamplugh Trust, which campaigns against stalking, is also increasingly concerned about spyware, drones and smart devices that link to phones.[11] Apple's AirTags, for example, can easily be slipped into someone's pocket to track them, and a report in *The New York Times* in December 2021 focused on the stories of several women who had been tracked and stalked in this way.[12] There are now many TikToks describing harrowing experiences like this. For example, @Angel Edge describes getting a notification on her phone about being tracked, but being unable to identify, let alone remove, the device that was tracking her, eventually turning off Bluetooth and wifi only to find the 'paired' object could still locate exactly where she was.[13]

More broadly, several participants felt that their devices and their apps were hyper-surveillant and intrusive – listening in to them, tracking them, generating extremely specific content based on facets of their interests and identity that they may not even be aware of themselves. Helena spoke about this at length:

> some people say I'm crazy when I say this, some people agree with me completely, I definitely think that our phones listen to us and take that information and throw up adverts and other content from what they can hear. So there have been times where I've mentioned something, without even using my phone to look it up on Instagram or any other app on my phone. And an advert for that will come up on my Instagram, which I find very unnerving.

And then also just from the way that the content that's rec-
ommended to me changes so quickly and specifically, according
to what I have been looking at, not even liking just looking at, I
find also scary because they just know so much.

Men don't get it

In the interviews conducted soon after Sarah Everard's murder,
fear of violence became even more prominent as a topic of
discussion. Sofia, 25, lived in south London close to where
Everard's body was found and she spoke about how angry and
how frightened she felt:

I . . . want to live my life and be able to go to Sainsbury's [super-
market] and not be terrified, do you know what I mean? As
well, it was very, very close to home. It was literally very, very,
very near where we live. So, that was a difficult time I think
when that was happening. I felt really weird those days actually.

Eve, in turn, spoke about how she identified with Sarah
Everard, and said 'I think the majority of women have had
some sort of experience . . . that interlinks with the Sarah
Everard case.' She had spoken with her boyfriend and his
group of friends at university about the case, and had been
shocked by their reactions, and by the discrepancy between
how they responded and how most women she knew felt.[14] She
explained:

I think they'd [my boyfriend and his friends] never do anything
themselves, I think they're very respectful of women. They're
not like one of these creeps in a nightclub who would grab
someone's arse, for example, they're not responsible themselves for anything like that.
But I think they wouldn't call things out if they saw it, if you
know what I mean? So say if they saw something happen to a

girl, I don't think they'd necessarily go over to help and things like that. So I'm not 100% sure of how much it's got through to them, to be honest. I'm quite doubtful that it's a lot. I think a lot of boys think well it's not me, so I've got nothing to do with it. (Eve, 21)

Nazanin, 18, had a different experience, and said that boys in her network at university were actively talking about what things they could personally do to help.

I know loads of male friends and stuff have posted comments that they've seen things that a man can do to make a woman feel safer and stuff. Which I think is brilliant. Good on men for making that awareness as a young man, but then, at the same time, this is again, this is a continuous thing. It's not all of a sudden going to stop now just because someone realized what was going on is wrong.

Across my interviews, however, Nazanin's experience of men actively posting in support was unusual. Sofia, 25, shared Eve's sense that men do not 'get it' at all. She described going out one evening with a man, who, as they were saying goodbye, told her that he loved to walk through the city at night listening to music:

I was on a date and he was like, I love after a night out when it's night just walking home and it's so peaceful in London, putting my headphones in and listening to loads of music. So peaceful. It's like meditation. You should try it.

In a tone of entirely justified outrage, Sofia told me how she responded:

I was like, you want me to at 3 AM walk through London on my own with headphones in as I'm walking down the street? That's your suggestion to me?! And he was like, what?? I was like, that's literally crazy! You can't do that! And he had *no idea*. It very much did not even cross . . . And he was not a person that was like . . . Definitely someone that considered themselves a feminist and he was someone that was very much women's rights but he had no idea. He just didn't even think that that would be a consideration for me.

In both these examples, Eve and Sofia are talking about men who are 'respectful' and 'feminist' yet who have simply no understanding of women's experience, or of the myriad ways in which women have to practise embodied safety strategies including careful route planning, keeping keys in hand, texting a friend, etc. Sofia described it:

If I plan to do something, my first thought is how am I going to get back? What time will it be? Will it be dark? Where am I going to have to walk? Will there be lights? It's just this rolodex of thoughts that you go through and I don't even think of it anymore. I just work it through, how am I going to stay safe?

The girlfriend gaze and peer surveillance: circuits of competition, cruelty and care

The final experience of feeling watched I want to consider is 'peer surveillance'[15] or what Alison Winch has called the 'girl-friend gaze' in which women watch and police each other.[16] Given how central this experience is to women's lives, it is surprising that so little research has explored it. Alongside Winch, Ana Elias is one of few scholars that has discussed women's experiences of being and feeling watched.[17] In her research in the UK and Portugal, she documented how young women felt themselves to be subject to almost ubiquitous surveillance. One of her participants, Simone, talked about feeling that on the (London) underground 'everyone is scanning you, like everyone is measuring you, taking my measures.' This experience offered few safe spaces – not even the changing rooms at the gym or pool. One woman described feeling that even in the most cursory 'glance' she was actually being 'x-rayed', that is deeply assessed. Another woman, Adriana, vividly expressed her experience of being subject to a 'checklist' gaze, in which other women would sweep up and down her body 'checking out' different features of her appearance:

> I experience it on a daily basis, I mean . . . If I happen to be at any given place and even with people that know me well . . . I realize that they look at you very often from head to toe in order to grasp how you look and if there is anything different in the way you look, kind of 'ok, hold on, let me check you out!' I understand that it is not malicious, most of the time . . . but . . . it feels almost like a checklist kind of 'ok you are approved, move ahead' . . . (makes gesture as if on a production line for robots).[18]

This judging observer is a lived emotional reality for many of the young women I interviewed too. India, 21, discussed the intense anxiety she felt about both posting to social media but also being seen out and about in everyday life, because of her feelings of not being attractive enough. In her case this centred on her eyebrows not being as full as she would like, making her feel acutely self-conscious:

> Well, I do that thing with my eyebrows [pulling them out due to anxiety]. So I've only got half an eyebrow here and the rest is not there, so I have to draw them on every day. I feel very self-conscious when I go out with my eyebrows not looking like they are eyebrows. So I'm very anxious about that. Yes. I'm not even sure if anyone would particularly notice or care, but I do know what people can be like with comments. Even if it's

just a passing comment, it still affects me because I just think, ah, yes, people do notice . . . Sometimes they just say it completely harmlessly, not thinking that they're making an impact at all. They might just say, look, she's not got many eyebrows, especially because these days, everyone is very into big, bushy eyebrows, so obviously not [overtalking], but I do know that girls can be quite bitchy with that sort of thing. Even just an acknowledgement would still make me very anxious about it.

Here we see clearly the dynamic in which feeling less than perfect, combined with having a sense of being under omnipresent critical scrutiny can be experienced as highly anxiety-provoking – even without the presence of 'comments'. Getting negative comments, as I discuss in chapter 6, was highly feared, and many young women undertook 'anticipatory labour' to try to avoid any negative or 'judgy' reactions. This was part of a culture of mutual surveillance and judgement, as expressed poignantly and eloquently by Bianca, 18, as she told me 'you might not see' that there's something wrong 'but *they* will':

I have to pick a background that I feel comfortable in and I don't want to show too much of my house because I don't want people to go ugh, is that where she lives? Or, oh, she's got a nice little. Just nasty comments. So, I try to keep it plain backgrounds. But just in general, you've got to be careful.

Like, I don't like my knees so I crop them out if they're in a picture. Because I don't want someone to say oh, you've got funny knees or something like that. So, you're a bit like you try to avoid those comments that you know people are going to say about you. So, before they even say it just avoid them and cut them out.

Checking with friends was a key way of dealing with such anxieties around posting. Most people told me that that they had two or three trusted people – a close friend, a sister – that they would show or send a picture to before posting it. Bianca, 18, told me that her older sister and her mum played this role for her. Bipasha, 23, said that she and her friends had evolved a special 'friend code' for giving feedback on each other's photos as there had been some hurtful incidents in the past when 'things had been said' and they'd 'had words'. So now: 'There's a rule between a few of us. It's you have to be honest, you have to say, yes, this is a good picture, or no, I've seen you look better in other pictures. That's how we phrase it.' In this way, friends were a source of support and solidarity.

However, friendship could also be a site of judgemental scrutiny, unkindness and competition. Lynne talked with me about her sense that the competitive dynamics of friendship contributed to the tyranny of the perfect, and put one at risk of failing if one did not live up to the standards – what she called 'the excellence' – of a friendship group. She explains these pressures vividly in the extract below, which is worth quoting at length:

Lynne: Yes, it's just, I think, maybe that whole perfect life thing comes from the fear of everyone talking about you. Because it's still quite competitive. And then you feel like it's a little community of achievers. You can see where your friend's doing really well. And people you used to know, or like, or you didn't even like . . .

So, if you're not putting more excellence into the excellence that they've already started, you just feel a bit like A, you're not good enough, or B, you are excluded from that group of all of these people who are commenting on each other's posts: Yes, you're doing really well. You'd really like to see this. You look great. This looks really interesting.

So, it's like you lose . . . if it's not an amazing post, if it's not perfect, you lose confidence in yourself. But you also lose connections to other people who are posting the perfect images as well, I think.

RG: Is it all domains of life?

Lynne: It's definitely more appearance. Because straight off the cuff, it is a picture, and it is yourself, and people are going to be looking at you. But, it's also if you're getting into university, you'll post a screenshot of look, I've been accepted into this university.

Or I'm going to say nights out. Pictures of your drinks. How many drinks you've got? Yes, it's just everything. If you've got a job, oh, first day at work. It really, I think it is . . . It covers everything. It's just you feel you constantly you have to update what you're doing and let everyone know.

You don't want them to look back and be like, oh, my gosh, I wonder what she's doing? Because then if you have got a group of people, a group of friends that you're talking to about Instagram, and you're doing fine and you're in there, it gives you the power to look on someone else and be like, oh, my gosh, what is she doing? We're all up here, what is she doing? So and so hasn't posted in weeks, and when she does post, she gets 20 likes. It's just exclusion in a really weird way, because you're not perfect, I guess.

A strongly classed sense of being perfect is conveyed by Lynne's words, though it should be noted that the experience cross-cut all identity positions. Lynne is a middle-class white student at a university with a very good reputation, and offers a clear picture of the pressures of 'keeping up' with a group of 'achievers'. In this way Instagram becomes a vehicle to display success of various kinds – an attractive appearance, a place at a good university, a night out in which the drinks are flowing, etc. – but also *itself* becomes a medium of success or failure – by not posting enough, or the right kinds of images, or by not accruing enough likes. Lynne's account here offers a vivid sense of the fear of falling down, and becoming a subject who can be judged a failure: 'oh my gosh what is *she* doing'. Lynne was highly critical of this: she found it morally and politically troubling and experienced it personally as utterly exhausting and draining. Yet to opt out or resist – to stop posting a perfect life – she explains, is to risk becoming excluded from a group of friends who are all doing this no matter whether it reflects their actual experiences. These dynamics of perfection and judgement, then – and of competition and care, of inclusion and exclusion – are *relational dynamics*, woven into the fabric of friendships and of wider peer networks, such as people you were at school with, go to university with or with whom you work. Whether or not one actually *likes* such people is surprisingly unimportant in terms of their power to 'judge you' – in fact I was told repeatedly of the very particular anguish of being judged by people you dislike and do not respect. What is operating, however, is a relational network of peer surveillance and judgement in which many are reluctant participants and most feel caught and isolated.

Lynne, like India and Bianca, feels enmeshed in a kind of 'surveillant sisterhood'[19] that is characterized simultaneously by affection and by 'normative cruelties'.[20] There is genuine care and there are relations of friendly, supportive advice, but there is also – sometimes in the same moment – competitiveness, mutual policing and a kind of 'warmly couched hostility',[21] sometimes expressed as 'concern', e.g. 'Are you really going to post that?' 'Don't you think you look too this' (where 'this' might be 'slutty', 'fat', 'drunk' – or something more specific about hair, makeup, clothes or venue). Young women, then, are not only watched, stared at and leered over by strangers and by men, but they also feel themselves caught in a web of forensic surveillance and judgement *from their peers and their friends*. This highlights both the ubiquity and intensity of their experience of being watched, and the complicated and ambiguous circuits of cruelty and care in which they feel entangled, even among their close friends.

Conclusion

This chapter has investigated a whole range of ways in which young women said they felt under scrutiny or that they were being watched. This criss-crosses both online and offline contexts and is both public and private, social and intimate, general and forensic. Scrutiny and judgement mark the contexts for interpersonal violence – including a level of harassment that should be horrifying yet is largely taken-for-granted – but also for the violence of a beauty industry intent on systematic pathologization and abnormalization of women's bodies, designed to make girls and women (and increasingly others) feel uncomfortable, insecure and like they are failing. Women felt subject to male gazes, racialized gazes, heteronormative gazes, classed gazes and gazes that centre on normative bodily appearance; they feel watched by technology companies and platforms; and they feel implicated in a web of peer surveillance and judgement, including the girlfriend gazes of their closest friends.[22] In the next chapter I turn to how they negotiate and manage this in their own posting practices, highlighting the time, energy and work they put into curating their social media.

5

The work of being social

I'd make sure my hair looked cute. I'd make sure that my body was looking good. I'd make sure it was from a good angle, like I'm make sure I'm sitting up straight rather than rolled over . . . yes I think about all of those things before I would take a picture . . . I would spend half an hour on one particular picture to make sure that I knew what looked good with that picture so that my body looked good. (Adija, 27)

Thus far I have discussed young people's social media practices; their experiences of feeling overwhelmed by images that are exclusionary, unrealistic and impossible; their new ways of seeing – inculcated by smartphone affordances, platforms and a rapidly expanding beauty industry; and their experiences of feeling under constant surveillance. In this chapter and the next, I turn to women's experiences of *posting* on various social media. I show how young women feel both 'hailed' and trapped by the perfect, and strive to present their own version of this in the photos they post. They do not unthinkingly follow what they see others doing, but rather adapt their appearance and creatively develop their own images in such a way as to foreground their 'best self'. Participants told me that a good post is 'a nice photo' – one that is 'flattering' but 'authentic', 'amazing' but somehow 'spontaneous', and should not appear to be (unduly) filtered or edited. As well as looking attractive, posts should also display 'coolness', a sense of fun and popularity. A good post means being 'positive' – no matter how one is actually feeling – as well as creating captions that are witty, self-deprecating and relatable. To post, then, is to create something that is thoughtfully and attentively constructed, but which can pass itself off as not being the result of any particular care, effort or design.

Young people spoke about several different kinds of posts they make. These included posts to 'show support' to a campaign or cause (e.g. BLM or LGBTQ+ movements), posts to demonstrate a particular skill, interest or hobby (e.g. pets, cooking, dancing, skating, interior design, crafting), and genres of posts such as 'the night out photo' or 'the holiday photo'. By far the most ubiquitous, however, was the individual photo of oneself, and for many young women, 'posting' – unless otherwise specified – meant posting a selfie. The understanding of a good post is shaped by the meanings given to particular platforms by young people – such as the ideas that Instagram is 'for best', Snapchat 'for your real friends', 'Facebook for family', etc., as discussed in chapter 1. It is also mediated by judgements that are simultaneously *aesthetic* (it has to look good), *affective* (it has to depict the right kind of feelings or dispositions) and *relational* (shaped by friendships that, as we saw in the last chapter, entangle care, competitiveness and sometimes cruelty).

The chapter starts by looking at what young women described as the pressures to 'post a perfect life' – one that is 'picture perfect' but also shows them in cool locations, doing interesting things and demonstrating or performing fun, popularity and the 'right' kinds of dispositions and attitudes. Then in the second part of the chapter I look at the sheer *work* involved in posting – the labour of choosing locations, outfits, taking photos that convey exactly the right look, and then editing, augmenting and producing those photographs to make them 'perfect'. A large body of research examines these practices in relation to influencers or microcelebrities,[1] but there has been less attention paid to 'ordinary' experiences and practices of posting. Here I argue that there are significant continuities between influencers' practices and those of the young women I interviewed (regardless of the number of their followers): 'upkeep of one's digital image requires extensive self-work';[2] it involves 'highly curated content that foregrounds a perfect lifestyle';[3] it depends upon 'hidden',[4] 'authenticity' and 'visibility' labour.[5] Like micro-celebrities,[6] the young women in this research sought to create appealing on-screen personas and intimacy with audiences, through 'continuous multiple uploads of performances of a private self'.[7] I argue that the intense labour that they undertake on their socials reflects Taina Bucher's idea of the social in social media as 'a doing', a set of effortful activities or labours.[8]

Posting a perfect life

Picture perfect

For women, posting is shaped by a relentless pressure to look your best. So many young women told me 'No one ever just posts a picture of just how they are'. As Eve put it,

> I just think there's definitely a pressure there. No one's going to post a photo where they're relaxed, they're not posed, and maybe they look a bit bigger or things like that.

Young women told me that they always thought carefully about what to post, and they had very clear ideas of what makes a good photo. At its most basic, this is a picture in which they are 'wearing a nice outfit' and in which 'my hair is nice' and 'my skin looks clear', 'my make-up looks good', and 'I'm not looking fat'. It also doesn't look 'fake' or posed, but somehow natural and authentic. It is the photo of you that you want to be out in the world representing you: attractive, happy, popular. For most, the requirements were even more stringent. Some explained that they will only take photos from one side or another, that they have to 'know their angles', and may only post a photo (or even take one) if they have on (false) eyelashes or fresh nails. Lily, 20, explains what a nice photo is for her:

> It has to be on this side [shows me], so this is my favourite side, I don't like pictures on that side. I usually like to have my makeup, so my skin can look better, with my eyebrows, and maybe my eyelashes. I don't actually usually take pictures if I just have mascara on. So I like to only take pictures when I have my eyelashes, I feel like they add more to the overall look.
>
> And probably if my hair is nice, and it's not in a ponytail, or a messy bun, or something like that. So just when I've done my makeup, and I feel good about myself. So that's when I like to take a picture, so I can kind of be . . . You know, look at it and think, oh, that is me, that is what I look like. I don't look *too* bad.

In turn Bianca, 18, says she has a kind of checklist she applies to each photo:

> So I have no bum type of thing. So, I get conscious of does my bum look okay? Or, because my eyebrows are light, it's like, do my eyebrows look okay? Do my eyelashes look okay? Does my hair look okay? So, there's a bit of frizz sticking up, I'll try and blemish it out or cut it out. Everything has to be perfect.

For Adija, 27, who was starting her own fitness company and had around 10,000 followers on Instagram, the quality of the photo had to be really good and the content had to have the 'wow factor':

They have to be of a certain quality. They have to be, you know I had to get myself a really good phone, a really good phone so that I know all of my pictures and videos are going to be 4K and I, it's almost like if the quality is not good, if the backdrop is not good, if it's not exciting and something that someone would look at and go, 'wow that's really awesome' then I know it's not going to get over a certain amount of likes, so I wouldn't bother posting it.

She explained that she is 'going through a no make-up vibe. I'm trying to go for a-fitness-and-empowering-women-to-not-have-to-wear-make-up – that kind of thing.' This means that – unusually – she doesn't spend time on cosmetics for her posts but this doesn't mean she posts 'just anything', and in fact it might create even more work to generate a good enough picture:

> Adija: I'd make sure my hair looked cute. I'd make sure that my body was looking good. I'd make sure it was from a good angle, like I'm make sure I'm sitting up straight rather than rolled over . . . yes I think about all of those things before I would take a picture . . . I would spend half an hour on one particular picture to make sure that I knew what looked good with that picture so that my body looked good. So I guess I would be editing in that way. I take one pose and take 40 pictures of it, check it and like, oh need to fix that bit, need to fix that bit kind of thing. So I would edit on that way.
>
> RG: So by redoing it, by redoing the action?
>
> Adija: So I'd go out, do a pose. Go back and check the picture and be like, oh I could have sucked my tummy in a little bit more. Go back, suck my tummy in a bit more, check the next picture and be like, okay that looks a bit better, but that one I need to arch my back more. Go back.
>
>   So . . . everyone will think you just do it like, ah once. But it's like half an hour of checking and rechecking.

Pressure to look perfect affected everyone, and has a particular punitive force for some disabled young people. Katie told me that she always airbrushes out her wheelchair or crutches from pictures as these in themselves make her feel that other people would judge her less than perfect.

> So, yes, I think it's just difficult. I feel like there's . . . Because of the expectation to be perfect, as soon as you have a medical condition, then I feel like that's it, you can never be perfect. Especially when people view you on social media. So, I think it's just easier to hide it. I also feel like if I use a medical aid, or whatever, or have one in my photo, I feel like I almost have to look *more* presentable and better. Which is really weird because I'm still me, nothing changes. It is like, well, I have to make up for something.

While Katie spoke powerfully of the painful feeling of having to somehow compensate or 'make up for' her disability by having even more perfect appearance, Letitia, who told me she struggled with her weight and also with a lifelong skin condition, also explained that feeling good about her appearance in photos was always ephemeral and could evaporate at any moment. She also conveyed what a long struggle it had been to get to a point of tentative self-acceptance:

> It's taken me a long time. I've always . . . My weight's fluctuated. It's always gone up and down in size always. So, some days, I feel really good. And then, some days, it's like, I pick an outfit, and one day it looks great. And I put it on when it's time to go out, and I'm like, I look awful. And it is happening, that thing of, you look on social media, and you could see someone in something that you really like. And then you get it, and you're like, oh, I look completely different.

Location, location, location

The pressure around posting was not only about one's personal appearance, but also extended to other features of self-presentation such as where you are, who you are with and what you are eating or drinking. 'Backdrops' were very important, as Adija noted. Anna told me that she would only post if she was somewhere 'cool' and Eve explained that's she would be more likely to post with food or drinks that look good:

> If I'm somewhere cool or something, then I'll definitely put a picture or Instagram story. Which sounds bad, but I don't know. It definitely is that kind of thing. I wouldn't post if I was just sat home doing nothing. But definitely if it was a cool place I would be posting a lot about it. (Anna, 21)

> Say if I ordered a cocktail at a bar and it had a fancy umbrella in it, or it was steaming, or it looks really nice, I'd be definitely more likely to post that than if it was just a beer in a bottle. (Eve, 21)

Many participants told me that going out to the right kinds of venues was essential to a good post. Bianca explained that it means giving attention to everything from food, drink, outfit, location, and even co-ordinating your clothes with the colour palette of the venue you are in. Above all, a post has to show you 'having fun' and 'it has to be perfect':

> So say if I go to a club, it's the thing where before you start drinking you've got to get a nice picture in the club so you can show that oh, I go to these nice clubs. Or I go to these nice restaurants. If you have your food and you're in a restaurant don't eat the food yet or don't drink the drink because you need to show oh yes, look at me I'm having fun and I'm in this posh

restaurant or I'm in a nice restaurant, it's a nice background. So, you always have got to make it look nice and you've got to look at the pictures before you're like okay, that's fine.

Like, cool. But it has to be a nice background. And I know people go to Embankment [or London's South Bank] to get nice pictures. And they can tag the location and more people see it and they get their outfit right. Some people colour coordinate with the backgrounds or whatever it is and it has to be perfect. (Bianca, 18)

The pandemic had changed expectations about posting, and most participants in the earlier interviews said that they were posting less because they weren't going anywhere. In some ways this diminished the pressures around constructing perfect posts, and, as discussed in chapter 3, many young women became involved in distinctive projects of aesthetic rest and self-optimization. In other ways, though, pressures were heightened precisely because there were so few opportunities to see others and to post, so each one became freighted with expectations. During a phase of lockdown in which people were allowed to gather outside in groups of up to six, Soraya described the considerable lengths to which she went to get ready to meet some friends in the local park, carefully choosing her dress and shoes, doing her hair and makeup and 'having a mindset that I might get a nice photo for my Instagram'. In turn, Adija's first trip out was following the murder of George Floyd when she took part in a large demonstration in London in support of the Black Lives Matter movement. As a young Black woman, she felt profoundly angry and upset, and she was passionate about attending the protest despite the lockdown. Yet even as she did so, she told me, she was consumed with anxiety about her appearance, worrying both about being 'seen' in public after two months at home, and about what she should post of herself from the demonstration.

I went on one of the Black Lives Matter marches and that was the first time that I'd, after all this lockdown, been in front of that many people. I was so stressed about my outfit for the days coming up to it. I was like, when I was on the march I was feeling like, oh God everyone looks really nice, you know I should have worn something else or, and that's not what I was there for.

But it was always in the back of my mind. I don't know I wanted to present my best self because I hadn't seen anyone in so long.

And then even when I saw my friends for the first time, I was thinking, oh my God are they going to think I've put on weight, or how do I look different or, have they put on weight, or have I? And that's something that you're thinking with your *friends* let alone even with a big group of people. So yes it's all the time [the awareness of how you look].

This is reminiscent of John Berger's famous analysis of women being the object of the internalized male gaze. He argued that it leads to a split form of subjectivity in which, even in their most powerful and all-consuming experiences – he gives the example of a woman crying at her father's funeral – women can never be fully without a sense of themselves as 'a sight', of how they appear to others.[9] Adija's account shows how deeply anxieties around posting have permeated and how even a protest of immense political significance does not automatically translate to a lessening of appearance pressures. It is not clear whether the gaze anticipated, feared and internalized is a male gaze, a white gaze or a platform gaze.[10] What is clear is that it is an attacking and punitive assault on Adija's ability to live and feel comfortable even as she attended a protest about the murder of another Black person.

Perfectly positive

Bianca's emphasis upon showing you are having fun captures another element of posting, namely the requirement to perform as happy and popular. This goes beyond appearance pressures, desirable locations and good-looking cool nights out, reflecting the way these pressures have extended into presenting a perfect self. As India put it, 'I know I keep saying it . . . it's just this expectation to be your best you all the time.' The pressure to be positive was talked about repeatedly by young women. Survey respondents wrote again and again about 'pressure to post the best bits' or 'the positive aspects'. 'I only post photos of happy, sociable times in my life', said one woman. Another said 'I always present a positive side of me, always dressed up and confident, however in real life that's not necessarily the case.' Below is one of many similar comments left on the survey which describe social media as a 'show reel' or a 'highlights reel':

> We post the highlight reel of our lives. People, including myself, rarely post anything negative about themselves on social media and this isn't a realistic perception of everyday life. Things go wrong but we only want other people to see the perfect bits. You can so easily make people think you lead this picture perfect life when for most people this is not the case.

Lynne, 19, spoke about this at length, telling me that she has times when she really feels low, and describing the juxtaposition between her own experiences with scrolling through Instagram and seeing only happy, upbeat posts. It makes her feel 'abnormal' and like she can never be herself, she said, but she expressed the feeling that she has to 'shut down' negative emotions and just 'keep contributing':

> I go on Instagram every morning, I don't see even one example of something like 'do you know what, I have had a really hor-

rible evening. I feel awful.' And then if it ever happens to me, I'm just going to shut it down and go on Instagram the next day and just keep scrolling, keep contributing.

She explains that sometimes – rarely – someone will do a 'real' post about how they are actually feeling, but that even these were the briefest of interruptions to the flow of positive perfection in which the tears were aestheticized, eyes never red nor faces blotchy, and with a swift return to the perfectly positive:

> OK so people will do it once in a while. People will be really positive on their accounts, and then one day come out and be like, oh, I'm still trying to be realistic with you all, here's a picture of me looking bloated. Or here's a picture when I was crying over something. And you're like, that's not even . . . The bloat is that big (makes tiny gesture with thumb and forefinger) and they've had *one* tear. And it just makes you feel abnormal.

She went on to describe the over-the-top and hyperbolic reaction that greeted such small transgressions or demonstrations that someone is 'human':

> The most worrying thing about it is that it's not even a constant thing. It's *tiny* episodes or *tiny* examples once every three months. And then people are like, oh, she's human, you can't say anything. But that is not what human emotion is, especially as a girl, especially as a teenage girl. You go through so much in one day.

The pressure to post a perfect life did not only operate as a global imperative, but also in micro-sites, and even in the spaces where some people turned for support with mental health problems. One young woman left the following comment on the survey, highlighting how the 'perfect image' even extended to anorexia, making her feel that 'other people with anorexia' are having an easier time with it than her:

> They present a perfect image. Actually I have anorexia and using social media to follow other people with anorexia makes me feel like they can have all the good parts [like people caring about them and looking skinny] without the significant physical health problems and without binge eating and purging.

Other participants similarly said that they felt pressure to post as happy and positive, regardless of how bad they were feeling, even though this contributed to their isolation, and a sense that they were not coping as well with their conditions as other people.

The labour of posting

Given the intensity of expectations placed on posting, it is not surprising that many women said that they dedicated considerable time, energy and money to planning their posts. This was most evident among the five interview participants who had large followings (10,000 or over) on Instagram, and who were paid as brand ambassadors or who received clothes, shoes, beauty or fitness products from brands in return for a minimum number of posts using or wearing the items. However, there were fewer differences between these micro-influencers and the other participants than might be expected, and, as I will show, the work that they put into posting was very similar for many participants. Three of the five (Holly, Eve and Nadine) had got into working with brands 'by accident' while at university. Adija had a different trajectory, built around her background in dance and her conscious attempts to position herself in order to get work in advertising, dance and theatre, while in parallel building a fitness company aimed at empowering women. In turn, Ayeshah built her modest fashion profile, with help from her sister.

Holly explains how it was for her:

In first year of uni, and second year, if we went on a night out, and bearing in mind we went on a lot of nights out at uni (laughter) we just took a photo of each other, as girls do before you go on a night out. And we just started doing that every night out. And then, after a while, we built up quite a lot of pictures on our grid, just of all our night out photos. And then, I think [major British fast-fashion brand] messaged her first, and then she started doing that. So then, I was taking pictures of her for [brand].

And then, other brands, as well, obviously saw that. [Major British fashion brand] . . . saw my posts, and I had other brands seeing mine as well, because I'd just got pictures in other stuff. And then, they'd send us stuff. It just went from there really. We just got more and more brands wanting to send us clothes. And it became a weekly thing. We would just take photos every week.

And then, we started venturing out from just night out photos, and we started getting photos in the street or at nice restaurants or bars or wherever. Places like that. And then, I've been doing it for two-and-a-bit years now. I still do it at the minute. I try and post, maybe, four or five times a week. And I just go out every week and just get four outfits of all the stuff that I've been sent, and just post that.

Holly explained the work of creating posts was animated by contradictory desires to be 'on trend' but also to stand out both in her own presentation and the 'backgrounds'. This was felt to be getting harder and harder as Instagram became saturated with ever more influencers, meaning that you had to follow what was trending, yet also be a little different. Nadine laughed with me about a contemporary trend for posts from derelict urban sites, particularly slightly menacing images of multi-storey carparks where she dragged her mum to take photos. Holly in turn joked about her wardrobe becoming much more colourful when she realized that there was a post-lockdown colour trend on Instagram that she needed to reflect in her posts. This light-hearted banter disguised an immense amount of work, which included careful scouting for locations, researching fashion, photographic and 'background' trends; creating outfits from clothes they were sent; and pairing these imaginatively with particular styles of hair or makeup and their own accessories (e.g. belts, necklaces, earrings).[11] There was also the work of taking the pictures which often included mothers, friends or partners, and frequently included taking 'millions of photos' and 'being a perfectionist', as well as the intense labour around post-production.

Much of this work was hidden or made invisible by the brands that were its beneficiaries[12] and was also often downplayed by the young women themselves. Hours or even days each week of researching, styling, travelling to locations, photographing, editing and uploading in different formats and to different platforms is mostly glossed as 'fun' or 'a hobby' – until it became 'too much' and began to take over young women's lives to such an extent that everything was about getting the picture, and they often weren't enjoying it any more. Nadine described how it became a 'chore' having to post so often, and also how it had begun to 'ruin' things that should have been fun – because everything became about getting the photo. She described reaching a crisis point when she was on holiday with some friends who were also micro-celebrities. She said she was expected to produce:

> just, like, over 100 photos. And it was just like too much especially when I'm used to going away with other friends and it was just more carefree and we were just having fun . . . I didn't want to take photos anymore. It just felt a bit like a chore and like we're not enjoying our time here.

Ayeshah also talked about the 'pressure' and the 'overwhelm' of producing content for her 85,000 followers while at the same time studying for a degree. This highlights some of the costs of the obligations of visibility, of 'putting yourself out there'.[13] Strikingly, similar patterns could be seen among many of the participants who did not have anything like such large followings or contracts with brands. Many young women described carefully researching venues for creating striking or beautiful posts, helped by an entire industry that charts Instagrammable locations and the best times to visit them (e.g. at sunset). This helped to shape their social lives and where they went, even *without* the requirements of brands, and in ways that would be adapted to different budgets and work-patterns. For example, getting some great photos in a gorgeous cocktail bar might be prohibitively expensive, but could be achieved by having pre-going-out drinks ('prees') at someone's home and then just having one cocktail while out and making sure that you get the goods in terms of pictures.

The group 'night out photo', which Holly said filled her grid, is another area of continuity between 'regular' social media users and micro-influencers. It has become so stabilized as 'a thing', and so tightly governed by generic conventions, that it has almost taken on a compulsory character. Lily explained how it works in her group of friends, describing the time and effort it takes, and how exhausting it can be:

You see people posting stories of them being out with their friends. And as soon as you're with your friends, you should feel like, oh, I need to take a picture to show I'm mostly with my friends. No, I'm not just by myself the whole day. That kind of thing. And I feel like instead of living in the moment sometimes, people just try to take pictures. So even before a night out, when we've gone out, always like, no, let's take a picture, let's take a group picture. Instead of . . . It can be quite exhausting. Someone will be like, I don't like myself in this picture, no I look bad in that picture.

And it just takes half an hour of the time, instead of enjoying yourself with your friends, you're just posing there for half an hour. Yes. So it just kind of takes away from the time where you can spend talking to your friends, and like drinking, and playing card games, or those kinds of things. Instead you're just against the wall trying to look slimmer, and pose, and stuff like that.

Lisa told me 'I hate it' and described often feeling like a killjoy on nights out when she questioned the need to get a photo:

It's annoying as well because sometimes I do feel like that person because I'm like, oh, it's so nice we're all together, we have to get a photo. And sometimes you turn up somewhere and you're like, I really can't be bothered, but you don't want to be that one person who's like, do we actually have to do this? Yes. We do.

Despite what operates as a friends 'code of honour' among young women about checking that everyone on a night out feels ok about how they look in a group photo, all the interviewees had stories of times in which they had been tagged in photos where they felt they looked awful. Some found this troubling but said nothing. Others challenged their friends. Eve reported saying to one friend very sarcastically 'Oh cheers: you look nice, but you've not considered what I look like!' Still others had evolved strategies to ensure that it did not happen regularly. For example, Ches told me how she made herself photographer-in-chief for her group of friends – as a clever way of getting to select which photos made the cut – allowing her to avoid showing what she perceived to be an unattractive bump on her nose:

Well . . . I mean for me it's I have a bump on my nose, so from the side you're going to see that, so I just wouldn't get pictures from my side. And often on nights out I would have the photos taken on my phone, so then I can decide what to send everyone else using the group pictures, so then I have no opportunity of them posting and me thinking, oh I hate this picture of myself.

Post-production: filtering and editing

Preparing a post does not end with the selection of a 'nice photo' that meets the exacting standards of young women. As noted in chapter 3, filters and editing software to 'augment reality' are intensifying appearance pressures and raising the stakes on what counts as a good enough picture to post. The vast majority of young women said that they edited their selfies at least some of the time, and/or applied filters to them, but said that they had to be careful not to look 'fake', which was a key way of 'getting it wrong' around which there was considerable fear (see chapter 6). The standards for selfies were felt to be the toughest – compared, say, with group photos, and at the top of the hierarchy were Instagram posts, which required more careful editing than (Instagram) Stories and or content on Snapchat or TikTok. As Bianca explained:

With Instagram I always edit my pictures. With Instagram it's a thing where people can zoom in on the picture and look at something, oh, she's got a bit of a spot on her head, or she hasn't done her eyebrows properly or she hasn't done her makeup properly. Or her room's a bit messy. Or it's just everything. The picture has to be perfect. If there's something random in the background you've got to edit out or just not post the picture at all. I also use Facetune, so it gets rid of my blemish on my face, I have for years. And I will not post a picture without. On Instagram it's always a makeup picture, always, it's never just a normal picture of whatever.

Many told me that themed filters were out of fashion or a bit 'tacky', while others said there were new trends coming onstream all the time – for example a type of 'grainy' filter. Others said they 'played around' to see what looked best. In the survey 90 per cent of respondents said that they filtered or edited their selfies before posting them. Many did so reluctantly, simply to meet an accepted standard because, as Bianca explained, 'the picture has to be perfect'. They also did so with the knowledge that in editing or augmenting their images they were feeding into the very tyranny of perfection that made themselves and others feel bad. They made it clear that they were not in favour of an entirely Photoshopped or Facetuned world; on the contrary they were very critical of what this did, but noted that it is difficult to withstand the pressure. It had become normatively required and thus participants felt answerable both for doing it, but also for not doing it.[14] The following comments were written in the survey:

> If everyone is editing their photos on social media then you feel more pressured to edit your photos so you don't feel like the odd one out, which then contributes to the problem.

> People feel pressured to look like the images they see in the media, even though these are often edited so are impossible to be replicated.

Even when expressed in the impersonal form – 'people feel' – it is clear that personal experiences are being discussed, as in the poignant example below from the survey's free comments:

> [People's] perception of what is considered normal has changed, making them believe that certain aspects about themselves are not normal and are strange or something unwanted or not deserving of love.[15]

The aspects of women's appearance that were most likely
to be changed were edits 'to even out skin tone', 'to brighten
skin' and 'to make teeth whiter'. Smaller numbers adjusted
their body and face to look slimmer or to have larger breasts,
fuller lips, thicker hair. Eyes and noses were also frequently
adjusted, and disliked parts of the body could be 'blemished
out', whether a spot, scar, eye bags or cellulite.

A striking feature of young women's discussions about editing their photos was the tendency, in most cases, to downplay
what was involved both in terms of the changes made and
the labour involved. A typical experience for me as an inter-
viewer was to ask someone how they prepared a photo for
posting, and then be treated to a long, detailed list of technical
interventions in which participants sounded like professional
photographers: 'well first I change the lighting, crop the image,
then adjust the saturation, tweak the colour balance, adjust
the brightness, delete or blemish out any problems', etc. only
for the interviewee to then conclude (without irony) 'so barely
anything'. Yet even this supposedly minimal post-production
work took at least ten to fifteen minutes per photo. For some
– such as Adija, Holly and Kirsty – it could take considerably
longer.

Bipasha was someone who really enjoyed styling herself
in different outfits, in interesting locations and with varied
makeup looks. She would plan with great relish her days out
with her mum or her boyfriend, the aim of which was to
create some amazing posts and to have a laugh in the process.
Bipasha stood out for the pleasure she derived from the whole
enterprise, and she walked me through what she does when
she has a photo that she thinks might be worth posting, and
thus worthy of editing:

> Basically I have Facetune2, the premium version, so I paid for
> it, and then I have VSCO. V S C O. I don't even know how
> you say it. But I don't know whether I did pay for that or not,

I'm not sure, but I *would* pay for it, so . . . Basically I'll go onto Facetune first. I'll get my picture, I'll press retouch and do auto, and then it will just clear my skin and change my skin colour a bit. It will just Photoshop me basically, and then I'll go onto the face bit.

If I think my nose looks big, I'll make my nose a tiny bit smaller. If I think you can't see enough of my lips, I'll make my lips a little bit bigger. I only do very, very small adjustments. I always look like me in my pictures because I don't want anyone to be like, she's edited them. My adjustments are tiny, but to my eye anyway it makes a difference. I'll always make my jaw smaller. That is probably what I do the most, is making my jaw smaller. I have a chubby face.

I might lift my eyebrows a little bit if I don't like my . . . If my expression's slightly off, I might lift my eyebrows a bit. If I've got red eye, I'll get rid of that. So, that's the retouch phase and then I'll save that, and then sometimes I'll go back and there's a separate section. There's a retouch section and then, I don't know, there's a separate section that you can do more of your face on.

Then I'll do conceal a bit more if my bags look a bit much. I'll matte my face a little bit because [unclear] a matte picture. I'll see if I can do my jaw even more, whiten my teeth if my teeth are showing. Then I'll save that and then I'll go straight onto VSCO and then I'll import the picture in. Then I do brightness up, contrast down 90% of the time, and then I will play around with all the different light adjustments, highlights, colours.

Then I will change the skin tone, because when you retouch on Facetune it makes it a bit too orange. It doesn't just quite look right. Yes, so then I'll adjust the skin tone to cool it down and make it look more like me, but a bit more golden. Then I will grain it all the way up. Not all the way. Sometimes. But I would say my last, between the last six and ten pictures I've used grain, and then I'm done.

As Bipasha talked me through her 'routine' she was animated and her eyes shone. She clearly loved doing this, revelling in the difference that small adjustments could make, and enjoying the satisfaction of her artistry, which seemed close to that of a professional. She said she was 'proud of my work'. She laughed a great deal, mock-worrying that what she does is 'so unhealthy' and 'really terrible', and jokily blaming it on her love of celebrity culture and of 'the TOWIE lifestyle'. She was extremely generous in sharing her experience, kindly offering to send me a video of her editing her face so that she could show me what a difference it made. Her enthusiasm was infectious – but it stood out as being different from the majority of young women's experiences.

Conclusion

This chapter has looked at experiences of posting to social media and the imperatives that shape it. It has explored the way that these are simultaneously aesthetic, affective and relational. Rather than seeing 'the perfect' as something abstract or distant or 'out there', it has opened up the everyday practices of choosing outfits and places to go, getting ready to have a night out, taking photos, and selecting and augmenting them, showing how these are conditioned by implicit and explicit notions of the perfect. The chapter examined pressures to be 'picture perfect' but also to post a 'perfect life' with photos from cool venues, exciting locations and nights out that establish one's sense of fun and popularity. It looked at the pressures to 'post the good bits' and to present a self who is happy, optimistic and positive. It also detailed some of the intense labour involved in posting to social media: from researching and planning, to taking multiple pictures, to editing and filtering them and uploading them to different platforms and formats, noting how the work of posting is downplayed and minimized, even for micro-influencers who spend many hours or days each week doing it. Drawing on a large body of work about the different forms of labour that micro-celebrities and influencers undertake – authenticity labour, aesthetic labour, relational labour[16] – I have argued that there are growing continuities with 'ordinary' social media users.

In the next chapter I situate the huge amount of work that young women do in maintaining their digital image in the context of their experiences of feeling judged and being fearful of 'getting it wrong'.

6

Fear of getting it wrong

*I remember I wanted to delete it [Instagram] for a bit because
of exams, and everyone was like, no, but if you do that then
people are going to think you've had a mental breakdown. That
you've completely gone off and you've disappeared. So, it's just
like every single action is just connected to some kind of fear or
anxiety. There's nothing you can do. (Lynne, 19)*

It would be hard to exaggerate the levels of anxiety that pulsated through women's accounts of posting to their social media. Even for those who relished planning and executing polished selfies, the process was fraught with anxiety. To post was to subject oneself to judgement from others, to forms of attention that might (hopefully) be kind and appreciative, but could also be hostile, cruel and forensic in their detail. Among my interviewees, Ruby, 27, was one of very few who seemed to approach the endeavour with unambiguous pleasure and joy, born of her brimming self-confidence and sense of comedy, and a level of comfort in her own body that came from her skills as a performer and acrobat. However, even Ruby admitted to occasionally feeling bad when she compared herself with others, and said she did not post images of her aerial

and acrobatic feats if she felt her tummy looked fat. She told
me:

> I'm friends with a lot of people who are just incredible, and
> they're amazing acrobats, and they're amazing dancers, and
> aerialists, and they're all in perfect shape. And they're all very
> skinny and muscular, and wear beautiful clothing, that sort of
> thing, and posting amazing things. And sometimes, I'm like oh,
> God, how can I possibly post when I'm compared to this?

Bipasha was another enthusiast who was exhilarated by
producing professional-quality photos with the help of photo-
editing software, but could also feel hurt and attacked by
negative comments. Ches called social media a 'happy place'
for her on balance, but posting could be the locus of considerable worry. For everyone else, experiences of anxiety, shame
and humiliation were topics that took centre stage, with the
sense of feeling judged as paramount. As 21-year-old trainee
animal welfare officer India put it:

> Honestly, it's awful. Every single thing anyone does is judged
> and I'm having anxiety anyway. It just makes things so much
> worse. I'm just anxious about every single thing I do now. I'm
> definitely influenced by the fact that it's going to be judged by
> people. Yes. It's very stressful because anything will be judged
> and you can't really . . . Even if you're just being yourself and
> people are all for being yourself, they're still going to judge you
> anyway.

In this chapter I explore the fears that young women
expressed about getting something wrong in relation to their
socials. I examine a wide range of both specific and incho-
ate fears. The chapter is divided into three parts. In the first
part, I discuss what young women said about the difficulty of
being 'perfect' while also being 'real'. This led to deeply felt

anxieties about being exposed as inauthentic or fake, to fears of being condemned for vanity, to worries about looking as if you are 'trying too hard', or anxieties about being seen as 'attention-seeking'. Next the chapter discusses likes, comments, screenshotting and trolling, highlighting a different set of fears about others' reactions. The third part of the chapter explores yet more ways that young women talked about getting it wrong: posting by mistake, posting too much or too little, and posting the wrong thing – for example, a 'bad' photograph or a statement or post of support that is later deemed inadequate or problematic in some way, such as the black squares which started as a gesture of outrage after the murder of George Floyd, but quickly became seen as a problematic act of 'performative anti-racism'.

Being perfect but also being real

At the heart of posting as an enterprise is what many young women experience as an impossible ask. As Lynne put it: 'I just think social media has got to a point now where there's this urge for everyone to be really realistic. And for everyone to be really perfect.' For participants in this research, this contradictory requirement generated multiple anxieties that many found extremely difficult.

Fear of being seen as filtered or fake

Young women told me that they felt under pressure to make sure that all posts were 'nice' and 'perfect' photos in which they looked their 'best'. However, some also said that there was a risk of appearing 'too' perfect and therefore seeming 'fake' or inauthentic. The fears around inauthenticity are another point of continuity between female influencers and other women on social media.[1]

Bianca worried about her pictures looking unnatural when she edited them or used filters:

> I don't want my pictures to look too fake, because that's not my Instagram, it's a bit like I want it to look as natural as possible, even though I'm wearing makeup. I want it to look like I haven't put a filter on or something like that [even when I have].

Anna told me that filters were 'out of fashion' and that they look too obvious and 'tacky' and 'false':

> I feel like now if you, it's out of fashion if you put a filter on a picture. Looks quite obviously like it's got a filter on it and it looks a bit tacky, maybe is the word. So I really don't like my pictures to look like they have a filter.

These concerns were shaped by a set of moral judgements around fraudulence, and ethical orientations towards authenticity[2] that almost all young women were committed to. Ches talked about editing her photos but in a way that kept them 'real'. She had a perception that her upper arms looked bigger in photos than they actually were in reality and thus she slimmed down her arms, while conveying a strong sense that this was not faking or 'cheating the system'.

> I'd sometimes I'd just use an editing app to make my arm look less fat, because if I've got it on my side I always feel like it looks big in comparison to how I know it actually is and so I feel like that editing doesn't feel like I'm cheating the system, it's not like showing something that isn't real.

Likewise, as we saw in chapter 5, Bipasha emphasized that although she heavily edited her pictures, she only made small changes and that it was crucial to her that she still looked like herself. In this context of ethical as well as aesthetic concerns,

Bipasha talked about how hurt she felt when someone commented that her pictures looked fake:

> Yes. I've had some nasty messages sent to me . . . One of them really upset me. Someone sent me a message saying, your pictures look more filtered than tap water, and it was completely . . . Yes, and that one upset me and I rang my boyfriend and I was like, why is this person saying this to me? He was like, they're literally just hating on you, babe, don't even worry about it, it's nothing, da-da-da.

Fear of being seen as 'catfishing' or overselling yourself

A related but slightly different fear was the worry that one would, perhaps through overzealous use of photo editing software, 'oversell' oneself on Instagram and this would lead to disappointment when someone met you in person. This was often spoken about in relation to dating, but it could also be an issue when one hadn't seen friends for a long time (as during lockdown). Lily discusses her fear of what she dubbed 'false advertising' of herself, and being seen as a 'catfish', and explains that this is why she does not undertake extensive editing or filtering of her pictures:

> No. No, I only do the exposure, so like brightness and contrast, just to make the quality of the picture better. But not necessarily edit any aspects of my face, because I feel like if people see that picture on Instagram, then they'll see me in real life, and I feel like it will be obvious that it's been edited. And, if anything, I feel like that will make me feel *more insecure*. The fact that I'll always be thinking, oh what if they think I'm a catfish or if I look very different than social media, in a way. So that's why I just try to post pictures that I like. They are the good pictures of me, but that is still me, so I'm not putting like a false advertisement.

Many others reported similar concerns along with statements such as 'people know what I look like so I don't want my pictures to look too much better'. Adija describes it as a problem in relation to her carefully curated fitness company image:

Adija: And also sometimes I do feel a bit of pressure when I've created this image of myself as [fitness company name], then I'll meet people in person and they're like, oh my God I've been following what you've been doing and then I'm sitting there thinking, oh I wonder if I look like what they thought I look like. Or if they're disappointed in my real self rather than this façade that I've been building. So that is definitely always something that you have in the back of your head without a doubt.

RG: Yes, it sounds like so much pressure?

Adija: It is yes.

Fear of seeming vain or looking like you are trying too hard

Another way of getting it wrong – rather ironic considering the immense amount of time women told us they spent preparing their photos for posting – is looking like you are 'trying too hard'. For example, Anna told me that another reason she wouldn't use a filter is because 'it looks like you are trying too hard if you do it'. Instead, you need to edit your picture to make it look 'like the colours are just amazing and it's a really good picture, kind of thing'. Here again there was an emphasis upon the spontaneous accomplishment of perfection, and the disavowal of anything that looked too much like you were trying.

It was interesting that several participants openly disclosed the strategies they used to not seem too vain or not appear that they have been trying too hard. Lynne said she would strategically embed a more perfect picture in a wider series of less flattering photos so she didn't look too vain:

If I look particularly nice in a picture then I'll put that up, but I try not to put just that . . . If I post a picture of just myself, I'll tend to make it like a series so that you can swipe through and there's pictures of other things, so I don't look as vain. There's a method to the madness (laughter).

Ruby, in turn, explained how she wanted to post amazing pictures and have people appreciate her, but didn't want people to think she was vain or 'up herself'. To offset this potential reading, she would deploy a self-deprecating, humorous caption that might – for example – ironically draw attention to her vanity:

I will say, actually, sometimes I *will* post these Instagram-perfect photographs. But normally, they will be accompanied by some sort of statement of me going I know I'm being incredibly vain here but look how fabulous I look.

I posted an Instagram story, where I was doing a handstand workout, and I walked past the camera and noticed how good my abs looked. And then spent a minute just going ooh, look at my abs. Ooh, they look great. Then be like, 'when you notice how good your abs look'.

Fear of being called 'attention-seeking'

As discussed in chapter 5, young women feel under intense pressure to post not only beautiful pictures but also a cool, interesting and happy life. In this context, as noted already, posting anything less than super-positive could easily make one a target for criticism. As many interviewees told me, posting was all about your 'best life', your 'highlights', your 'showreel'. If you posted while you were ill, sad, upset or struggling in some way, this would often be viewed as 'attention-seeking', something that Lynne discussed, when she highlighted the juxtaposition between her own emotional life and the sight of

so many shiny happy people who never seem to feel low. Lily
also brought this up. She remarked:

> Yes, I just feel like you . . . You never see someone posting when
> they're feeling down. You'll never see someone post a picture
> of themselves being upset. And if they do, people will just call
> them an attention seeker, or all this horrible stuff, you know.
> So I feel like everyone always tries to show, you know, look, I'm
> with my friends, or I'm out in a nice place. And instead of just
> posting a picture when they're at home, or when they're having
> like . . . You know, not feeling so well. And I feel like that's why
> it's just really bad. You just feel the pressure.

Young women explained time after time that, as one put it
clearly (on the survey): you 'don't show the downs, the hard
times because its seen as looking to get sympathy and can be
seen as playing a game to get more popularity'. Another wrote:
'I don't like to post everything about my life on social media,
for example bad or sad times as I don't want to come across as
an attention seeker. I only post good or happy times so some
people can see I'm doing okay and I'm happy.'

Many participants discussed how hard this could be, how
it prevented them from being able to be real or authentic
about how they were feeling, and kept them trapped in
posting glossy images of perfection, regardless of how they
actually felt. This was particularly tough for anyone who was
struggling with anything (e.g. a break-up, a bereavement or a
hard time at university or work), who felt that this had to be
silenced or erased. It is striking that even though there has
been much discussion of a 'turn to vulnerability' in recent
years,[3] being seen to be vulnerable remains a site of privilege,
and was not something that young women felt safe to display
on their social media.[4] Eve was one of several participants who
suffered from anxiety, and had also been diagnosed with an
eating disorder while she was in her early teens. But she told

me she would *never* post anything relating to mental health struggles for fear of getting a 'bad reaction' and being called 'attention-seeking':

> I think especially in terms of things like mental health. When people are honest I don't think they'd probably always get a good reaction, which is quite sad to think. I think some people, not to their face necessarily, but I can imagine some people would be like what is she gaining from that, she's attention seeking. I've never uploaded anything negative, just because I'm too conscious of doing that, but I think that's just one example where you might get a bad reaction.

Other participants with mental health challenges mentioned this frequently, as did those who saw themselves as less close to normatively desirable female appearance, for example those who were larger, suffered from visible skin conditions such as acne or eczema or had an obvious disability. For Katie, who was finally diagnosed in her late teens with a rare painful condition which took many years for doctors to identify, it exacerbated years of being misunderstood and being accused of 'faking' her pain and disability:

> RG: Can I just go back to one thing that you mentioned, which was you said that even though you don't post very often, that if you were posting, that you might even edit out your crutches if you were using them?
>
> Katie: Yes.
>
> RG: Could you say a bit more about that?
>
> Katie: I think I'm worried it'll come across as attention-seeking. I think that's the biggest thing. I was never really open. Most of my family didn't really know much about my stuff. And I think because it took so long to get my diagnosis, I didn't want to put things out there. And then people go well, what's wrong with you? And then I have to go I don't know.

Because then it's like loads of questions and that's when it's like, well, you're faking it.

When I was at school, I used crutches, but even then people would say oh, you're faking it, a lot. But then, even doctors have said that. So, I think I'm so worried to be open about it just because of the backlash of that stuff. So, I don't know, I think a post medically, is always coming across like an attention thing, or people think you're faking.

So, then, that's when I'm like, if I do post my crutches or my wheelchair, what good will come out of that? And then, really, there is none.

These cumulative experiences led to Katie deciding to try to live up to social media requirements and to not post images or captions that would be dissonant – even though doing so meant suppressing some key features of her own experiences and reality, which was a deeply alienating experience. It added an extra layer of suffering and isolation to her life. Not only did she feel unable to post about the particular difficulties she faced as a young, working-class disabled woman, but, on top of this, she felt in fear of being attacked for being 'attention-seeking' if she were to speak about or represent the reality of her life. She thus decided to say nothing. Yet the costs of being what Katie described as 'hidden', 'a hidden person', were also painfully high. The fear of being called an attention-seeker exerted a profound disciplinary force on Katie, on Lynne, Lily, Bianca, Letitia and many other young women. For some participants – such as Helena and Sofia discussed in chapter 1 – it contributed to them deciding not to post at all.

Likes, comments, screenshotting and trolling

Young women also felt deeply anxious about others' reactions to their posts. These included likes, comments, shares, as well as worries about their posts being screenshotted or trolled.

Fear of not getting enough likes

As we have seen already, young women felt under intense pressure to get 'likes', positive comments or shares for their posts, and an almost universal anxiety was the fear of not getting 'enough' likes – even though what counted as enough could vary widely. The likes economy was a means they used to assess and judge others – whether friends or potential dates, but it also reflected on how they saw themselves. Elizabeth, 23, told me:

> I don't want to post something which not many people like. And I know cognitively that's ridiculous and that it doesn't really matter, but people do notice if you get a lot of likes, and it always becomes a bit of a pressure really. I generally get quite a lot of likes on my profile pictures, but it's more just because I know lots of people and lots of people know me, and it's not necessarily because of the photo itself. But I guess it's a bit of a sign of popularity, and I guess I don't want to, I don't know, let that image down a bit.

Like Elizabeth, Holly was somewhat embarrassed to care about likes. She felt she should be able to get enough satisfaction from knowing that it was a good picture and feeling happy with it herself, but she explained that though she tries not to care, it makes her feel down:

> I don't really care if one photo doesn't get a lot of likes. It might just make me feel a bit down, because you've put effort into making the content, and going out there and making it look good, and making it look nice. And then, you feel like you don't really get the support back from people.

Adija, 27, compared the focus on likes and ratings to dysto-
pian dramas, most notably Charlie Brooker's 'Nosedive'[5]:

> It's like *Black Mirror* . . . you have your phone up and you get,
> you can rate someone. Like you would rate an Uber driver on
> there. You do it for people, and that's exactly what likes is on
> Instagram. Lots of people I know, they'll post something and if
> it doesn't get over a certain amount of likes they'll just delete it.
> Because it's humiliating.

These observations highlight the potential shame and
humiliation involved in not getting enough likes, the way it
offered a public review of one's popularity (or lack thereof).
Eve said that she would delete a post if it did not get at least
150 likes. Others with large followings set the numbers higher:
at 300 or 400. Katie confessed to ways she and her friends
would seek or had sought to generate more likes – even
though they might be 'fake', they offered a public affirmation, and a defence against the terrible shame of – as Lynne
put it – 'posting something that only gets 20 likes'. Katie
explains:

> I think it's still that bit where you're putting out everything has
> to be perfect on Instagram, I feel like. And it's always measured
> by how many likes you get. That's one of the big things. A lot
> of my friends will post a photo [on Instagram], and then they'll
> message me on Snapchat or something saying, oh, I've posted
> a photo, can you go like it? And it's just like everybody is so
> obsessed with the amount of likes they get.
>
> Even I am. When I was, I think, 14, and I was so worried that
> everyone at school was getting more likes than me. I had this
> app thing. So, you would go through it and it would give you
> people like you for being on this other app because you like
> other people's and they like yours.
>
> So, I think it's really bad that at the age of 14, I was actively

trying to seek likes that were fake, just so other people would think better of me.

Katie said 'it feels like a competition for proof that you are worth something' – even if it has to be faked. Like other participants, she is highly critical of this, regards it as 'really bad', but feels trapped within it.

And I think Instagram is the one where it's them trying to prove they're good enough by getting reinforced by the likes. But it's just not healthy.

But I think if everybody just didn't fake themselves and make themselves look perfect I think it would be loads better. But it just feels like a competition, almost.

After posting, young women would adopt one of two strategies: either, like Eve, Lisa and Soraya, they would repeatedly refresh the app to see how the post was being received, or, like Lynne, would become paralysed by fear and turn the app off completely because 'I'll be too scared even to look'. Eve said:

I know for myself, well for my friends as well, I've seen them all when I'm sat with them. When we all post a photo we'll be looking at that for hours afterwards, just clicking back on it and looking at it, not even to make sure it's okay, it's just to see how many likes it's getting or whatever.

And definitely say I posted the previous evening, when I wake up the next morning the first thing I do when I go on my phone is check how many likes it's got.

Fear of being trolled

A fear of getting negative comments, or, worse, of being trolled, struck dread and panic into young women. At the time of her interview, Anna, 21, had been involved in a BLM-inspired campaign to change a local street name from one that memorialized a colonial figure. She described her campaign posts receiving large numbers of very hostile comments, which had given her an insight into what trolling could be like.

> Just the glimpse last week of just having to deal with all the messages from the campaign, even though it was not that much, and it wasn't personal at all. It was still a bit stressful. I can imagine how awful it must be if you're getting that on a personal level.

Bianca, 18, discussed a different kind of trolling. She felt very angry at the sexual double standards that operated on Instagram, and the way that 'women always get blamed'. She expressed her terror that her ex-boyfriend might publicly post pictures which she had taken for him, to get back at her. Using her hands, her face and her voice, she conveyed being distraught and on the edge of a panic attack by the 'whole fear factor of that'. Over and above this particular possibility, Bianca felt subjugated by double standards that required her to post pictures in which she looked sexy, but that could easily be used to attack and slut-shame her too. She explained that this had happened to her while she was at school, and how devastating and unfair it is:

> For women I would say if you put a revealing picture up there, like if you're in lingerie or whatever, you're just showing a bit of cleavage people will view you as a slag, you're easy, you're a ho, you're a this, that. And people start making up rumours about you. That's what used to happen. . . . If I were to show my cleavage, it doesn't make me that because you don't know who I am. That's the thing with social media, you don't know who I am, only my close friends know. But people that are random will just think the worst of you and a picture can go viral within minutes, seconds.

Bianca explained that even if you take down the image that has caused all the 'hate' and 'blame' and the attacks on you, it will probably already have been shared via screenshots among your networks, and possibly more widely:

> Because on Instagram they can make Instagram pages where they do baiting out skets. And people will send in pornographic images of you or nudes and they'll [inaudible] with it. And that's it, you're on there. It's not so bad when it's other people on there, but when you're on there, it's bad and you're like *gasp* (gasps in distress).

It is hard to overstate the combination of anger, fear and powerlessness that Bianca communicated. She was enraged by sexual double standards, by slut-shaming, by the power of others who do not even know her to judge and condemn her, and she was also terrified that this might happen again at any time and that she would not be able to do a thing about it. Her experiences reflect a reality in which Black women are disproportionately subject to hate and harassment online.[6]

Fear of hostile screenshotting

One thing that made this particularly anxiety-producing for many participants was the sense of their images or photographs having an afterlife that they could not control and might not even know about, and that this may not just involve strangers or unknown trolls but might include close friends. Many of those with public or business accounts on Instagram (even if just to host university work, or show pictures of their dogs) had access to the 'insights' feature which allowed them to see how many times something they posted was reshared. Several said this made them nervous. Eve explained:

I think some things can make it worse on Instagram as an app in particular. When I was on a public account, and not private, there was a thing that I turned on where it allowed you to see how many people had sent your posts to other people. So that could make me feel very like oh I'm not sure, what are they saying about the post, it just feels a bit weird. That's another reason why I went private.

Here, again, is a continuity between 'ordinary' social media users and influencers, more and more of whom are moving to private spaces and changing to subscription models of earning from their content (e.g. Patreon).[7] Lynne said a little more about this feature and how anxious it makes her:

Instagram has got a new feature where you can track what happens. Track the actions taken. So, public, then you see if it's been sent to anyone else. Or if it's been saved. And it's just stuff like that. It's just so weird to think about. I wouldn't even get those features because I think it would just make me so anxious to use Instagram. But it probably would change how I used it as well and the kind of stuff I'd be posting. But yes. It's just so horrible.

Lynne explained the anxiety she feels after posting anything, making clear, as in discussions throughout the book, that a big source of the fear relates not to strangers but to *other girls in her friendship group* who will be carefully scrutinizing her pictures:

Yes, it's just like that weird fear that you get whenever you post anything. It's like I feel anxious, you're waiting for people. And it's not even because . . . I don't even . . . It's because am I going to get likes, am I going to get comments, it's not even that. It's I wonder if anyone is going to screenshot this and send it to other people. What they're going to say about me behind my back.

I asked Lynne if she had experienced this and she immediately offered a vivid account:

Lynne: Sometimes it's not direct comments. Someone might Snapchat you or message you about what you've posted. And saying oh, why did you post that, or don't you think that's a bit revealing. Or don't you think you look too this or too that. And then you might feel a bit outside.

But if you're in a friendship group, especially with girls, they're probably not going to put it on social media because they don't want everyone else to see it. So, it's more behind closed doors. But it's the same kind of comments, I think.

RG: God. Could you give me an example?

Lynne: Well, I don't know if I can say it ... You know like [those girls I mentioned], we'd all be in group chats and they'd send screenshots of other people's profiles into the chat. And be like, oh my God, this is definitely edited, or look at her legs, or look at how this she looks. Or they'd send you yours and be like, oh, really, you're going to post this now?

You'd have to send what you were going to post, as well, to them first for them to be like, no, you shouldn't post that. Or you should do this. It's definitely more of small friendship groups just commenting on each other.

The many other ways of getting it wrong

Night-time posting

Posting at night or after having drunk alcohol held particular anxieties for young women. Among Snapchat users, an almost ubiquitous fear was the anxiety that they might accidentally post something that they had not intended to share – because the 'capture' button is right next to the 'share' button. As 20-year-old Ches explained:

In terms of making stories and stuff, I do have an anxiety over
... I don't want to accidentally post a story or whatever, just
because the way you can post a story is very easy to happen,
it's just one button when you're taking a picture ... the button
next to capture is post, so it seems so easy, even though it's
never really happened, it just feels like it's so easily done.

Alba had the same worry:

I've done that before on a night out and it's horrible. So yes I
have a lot of anxiety about doing that. But I think a lot of people
do, it's quite natural to, and it's easy on Snapchat to accidently
put something on your story. Easier than it is on Instagram or
somewhere.

Many participants said they were kept up at night by worries about this or that they would check their phones *multiple
times* before going to sleep to make sure that they hadn't accidentally posted something, miscaptioned something, shared a
photo that was not good enough or otherwise put themselves
at risk of negative judgements. Several told me that their night-
time checking of their phones cost them sleep, and verged on
what one described as 'OCD' as she repeatedly checked that
she had not made any accidental or poorly judged posts. She
would then put her phone down in order to sleep, but then
had to check again and then again until the anxiety abated.
Young women described hearts racing, adrenaline pumping
and experiences of absolute panic. Several others said they
deliberately avoid posting at night as it causes too much anxiety. As Bianca, 18, explained:

So, also, say ... mostly what I do, on Snapchat, I'll *delete* a
picture before I go to bed. Or, I don't post before I go to bed
because I'm scared I'll wake up in the morning and it's got the
wrong interpretation or there's something in it that I posted

and you see all these messages and you're like why have I got all these messages? And you start panicking, everyone starts popping up to you, you're like oh god, it's really scary. I don't post when I go to bed. And I check several times, clear all my messages, everything.

Fear of posting too much or too little

Another widespread worry related posting too much or too little. Both, it seems attracted opprobrium and shaped social media practices. Young women told me they were anxious about annoying people by posting too often and that there was a need to 'regulate' how often you appeared in others' feeds:

> Yes, I don't really like to spam people in a way. I feel like it gets kind of annoying if you just constantly see someone's face on social media if they post too much. So I kind of try to avoid just posting anything that's going on during the day. And also I don't usually take a lot of pictures. I just kind of do it if, as you said, it's a night out. So I've done my makeup properly. Or I look nice, and I feel kind of good about myself. I don't just take any pictures, and just post anything. (Lynne, 19)

> But for me I just wouldn't ever post that often anyway even if I had a lot of photos because I think I just wouldn't want to keep appearing on someone's, I wouldn't want to be an annoying person. Even if I had loads of photos to post I think I would still somewhat regulate how often I post them just so that I'm not bombarding anyone with pictures of me. (Soraya, 20)

However, they also felt a pressure to post 'enough' for fear of being seen as anti-social or being forgotten. Lynne described how stopping posting might make people suggest you've 'had a mental breakdown'. At one point when she was studying for exams, she wanted to take a break from her social media, but

then had to endure critical comments about her absence –
often, she said, expressed as 'fake concern' about her mental
health. Bianca had similar experiences and told me that having
people check up on you after a silence could be nice, but it
could also be 'judgy':

> On Snapchat the longest I haven't posted is two weeks, a week.
> Because people start asking, where have you been? I haven't
> heard from you or oh, you're always posting, where have you
> been? And you're like oh. Or you're being antisocial and you're
> just like, I'm just trying to get on with it.

Lily explained that towards the end of lockdown – after
a period in which few people had been going out and, cor-
respondingly, the number of posts had dropped dramatically
– there was more 'pressure to post' building again. It was striking how frequently social media engagement was characterized
as an obligation rather than a pleasure:

> But I do feel like there has been a bit more pressure to post
> and stuff recently. Because now people are kind of seeing their
> friends again, so it's like oh, people are actually doing stuff. And
> I do kind of feel like I *should* be meeting my friends, I *should* be
> more active on social media again, that kind of thing.

Fear of posting the wrong thing

A different fear expressed by participants was the worry about
saying or sharing the wrong thing on their socials. While, so
far, we have largely talked about images, this related also to
text that was posted. It might be a matter of using the wrong
'tone' in a caption and coming across as arrogant, or it might
be the fail of sharing something that was just slightly 'off' –
perhaps it had been overshared or it was not quite the right
resource to share. Concerns about 'call out' or 'cancel culture'

are often characterized as emanating from the most privileged in society, who, far from being silenced, have access to significant cultural space and voice. However, in these interviews with diverse young women at the start of adulthood, precisely these concerns about being called out were evident. As one Black young woman told me, there's a sense that people are poised ready to pounce on you; they *want* to 'twist up your whole words', she said. I was asking if social media felt like a safe space:

> I don't know. I feel like what I told you, you think back and you're not safe on Instagram and Snapchat. You say one little thing and someone can misinterpret it like crazy. You can be like oh, I don't like white t-shirts. People will be like you don't like white? Oh, so you're racist? They can twist up your whole words. So, you try to [inaudible], you can't say anything. I remember I said I don't want a black controller for my [unclear], I want a blue one now. And someone went what do you mean you don't want a black one? You're racist.
>
> And I was like, how am I racist? . . . So, you've got to be really careful on what you say, because it's always a trap (Bianca, 18)

The fear of saying something wrong cross-cuts a number of different scenarios, but was particularly evident in this research in relation to #BlackLivesMatter activism because of its heightened visibility at the time. As I documented in the Introduction and chapter 1, almost everyone who took part in the interviews expressed enthusiastic support for the #BlackLivesMatter movement; several interviewees had taken part in protests and demonstrations during the weeks I was interviewing and all were active in expressing solidarity, and seeking to educate themselves and others. As should already be clear, several young people of all heritages and ethnicities considered political activism, and particularly #BLM, as one of the most important reasons for being on social media: as a source of alternative information from mainstream media, as a way of displaying support and as a tool for education. Moreover, many were highly articulate about the nuances of online participation – they spoke eloquently about the dilemmas of 'silence is violence' versus 'performative anti-racism'. They debated out loud worries about sharing information that might be 'triggering' for some; they expressed anxieties that certain gestures might merely be a form of 'virtue signalling'; in short, they demonstrated subtle understanding and awareness of a variety of issues at stake. Nevertheless, they also experienced quite significant fears about 'getting it wrong', of inadvertently saying something that would draw censure and possibly erasure.

In an extract that is typical of several discussions in the interviews, Lisa, a 20-year-old white woman who was a passionate and thoughtful supporter of #BLM, describes how her anxiety about doing something wrong on social media eventually caused her to delete Instagram from her phone:

> So with #Black Lives Matter, obviously it's a really useful resource to find stuff, but I got really caught up in people saying, you need to post this and share this information, and people saying, if you post this, you're being performative antiracist, and I was just spending all day going, is it bad if I don't post this, or . . .? So I deleted it because it wasn't really productive.

She elaborates with a focus on Blackout Tuesday, which started in the US music industry as a protest against the murders of George Floyd, Breonna Taylor and Ahmaud Arbery but quickly became a worldwide phenomenon on social media:

> When everyone was posting the black squares, I remember the day that came out I was so worried about whether . . . Because I never normally post . . . I post three times a year or something. I don't really like posting that much, so I was like, I don't really

want to do this, but obviously, if it's going to help, then I should do it. And everyone was posting stuff like, if you're staying silent, we can see you, and stuff like that.

And then the next day everyone was saying, this is completely useless, it's just a token thing, and everyone that posted it was getting their friends saying, why did you do that? So it just felt like you ... And also, I'd rather be doing actual educating myself or donating money or something like that than spending all day worrying about what's the right thing to post.

Lisa was also well aware that her own 'agonizing' on this issue was itself an index of her privilege as a white person. She told me 'Obviously if you're Black then you have to confront racism every day. So it's a bit ... I'm not complaining about the fact that I have to think about it more often.' Rather she was thinking seriously about what it means to be an 'ally' in more meaningful ways than posting a black square.[8] Her dilemma should be understood in the context of a moment in which many people experienced 'a felt imperative to "take a stand"'.[9] Tanisha, 26, was also involved in antiracist activism but had concerns about 'what to post' or 'whether I'm just posting to post'. She expressed myriad different feelings about it: she feared the weight of responsibility, of being someone that 'people look to'; she also feared accidentally trivializing an issue when 'it's really serious and then the next frame of my story is look at me eating ice cream'; and she feared backlash and criticism, and, like Lisa, said that she would rather be 'reading about these topics and having discussion with people in real life'.

Fear of losing friends

What came across clearly from the interviews – on all topics not just BLM – was an at times paralysing fear of judgement in a climate on social media in which people are felt to be quick to criticize, condemn and dismiss. This operated globally as a fear of being 'called out', but it also operated locally in intimate networks of friends and acquaintances, which for many of my participants could be very large: their actual friends, large numbers of people they knew from school or university or work, the friends and networks of those people, and so on. This resonates with Loretta Ross's argument about 'calling in the call out culture'.[10] She contends:

> Call outs are justified to challenge provocateurs who deliberately hurt others, or for powerful people beyond our reach . . . but most public shaming is horizontal.

Two young women shared with me deeply painful experiences of losing friendships via misunderstandings on social media platforms, which then escalated and 'got out of hand', and from which there was 'no way back' because of things that had been said. Even without a catastrophic ending, many told me that there was a need to be *incredibly careful*, as small things could cause great hurt and friction – for example being on the app and not liking a friend's post, or leaving a nice comment on one friend's picture but not on another's. The need to be constantly attentive to all these potential slights and microaggressions contributed to the sense of overwhelm so many described.

Many participants drew stark contrasts between conversations in their offline worlds in which they felt there was far greater understanding of their points of view, the chance to explain and ask questions, and less tendency to hostile judging, and exchanges online which were ripe for misunderstandings. I asked Bianca to explain:

RG: Yes, do you feel like that in real life as well? Or is it just on your socials that you feel that need to be careful?

Bianca: It's mainly on my socials I have to be careful. As when you're face to face with someone you can confront the situation more. Like no, I didn't mean that, you know I didn't. Whereas with social media, you can't bring emotion to it as much, people will be like she's faking it. Because when celebrities say something, they come with a video saying I'm so sorry for what I've said, people are like you're lying. Whereas when you're more face to face with someone you can just deal with the situation.

Whereas on social media you can't. People start mixing up your words, it's crazy.

Conclusion

This chapter has explored the intense vulnerabilities that young women feel about 'getting it wrong' on social media, particularly in relation to posting. The experiences of feeling subject to impossible standards of perfection, and of feeling watched and judged, culminate in the anxieties documented in this chapter, which were not only extraordinary for their sheer number and variety, but also for the palpable fear they generate. The chapter looked at anxieties relating to the need to be 'perfect' but also 'real', centred on fakeness, vanity, trying too hard and being attention-seeking. It also looked at anxieties relating to likes and shares and other forms of engagement or ratings. It discussed the concerns participants expressed about being subject to trolling, image-based abuse or hostile screenshotting practices. And, finally, it considered the myriad other ways that young women felt they could 'get it wrong' on their socials – such as by posting too much, too little or posting the wrong thing. While this chapter – and indeed the book as a whole – has demonstrated how thoughtful, active and creative young people are on their socials, this chapter has demonstrated that being 'savvy' or 'sophisticated' does not magically erase difficulty or distress. It has shown vividly the dilemmas and struggles that young women experience, and that alongside experiences of fun and connection are powerful anxieties about social censure, humiliation and shame. It is the task of the concluding chapter to draw together these threads.

Conclusion: Feeling judged

No one really talks about how hard this is. I think we are all just expected to cope with it. (Letitia, 27)

Perfect: Feeling Judged has documented young people's lives on social media, with a particular focus on young women's experiences in the early 2020s within converging crises. The book has highlighted the ambivalence, contradictions and struggles that characterize young people's experiences on and with social media. I have looked at experiences of pleasure and fun, inspiration and motivation, and connection and community. When things were going well, some participants said 'I absolutely love it' (Bipasha, 23) and talked about the thrill of 'knowing what is happening' (Sofia, 25), 'sharing experiences' (Ches, 20) and 'feeling part of a community' (Alex, 20). Much more often, though, young women described 'how tough it is' (Bianca, 18), or 'how hard it is' (Letitia, 27). What made posting on social media difficult, young women told me, is the particular force of the requirement to live up to – and produce in your own photos – a perfect version of yourself and your life, while being subjected to never-ending forensic scrutiny, judgement and harassment – and not being allowed to fail. As Adija, 27, said of her social media experience: 'It's like an episode of Black Mirror, but this is actually real life!'

As I noted at the start of this book, the research took place at an extraordinary moment marked by 'polycrisis'[1] – pandemic, lockdowns, war, austerity, the start of Brexit, institutionalized racism, sexism and disablism, a collapsing health and social care system, and dramatic losses in public confidence in government and other institutions (particularly the police).[2] Many aspects of this wider context came to the fore in this research – particularly experiences of poverty and unemployment, and the grief and rage provoked by police racism and brutality and sexual violence. Nevertheless, this 'extraordinary' time was also a period of 'ordinary' life, and the questions that animated my participants were at once more intimate and more existential than a focus on crises might suggest: how to be, how to present oneself, how to manage friendships with different degrees of closeness, and perhaps above all, how to survive and get by in social media spaces that could be difficult, challenging and toxic.

In this concluding chapter, I will draw together the arguments that I made in this book including discussing the emotional landscapes that young women discussed, looking at the disturbing levels of anxiety, shame, depression and exhaustion expressed by so many participants. The final part of the chapter discusses how young people are managing these challenging social media lives, and looks to the future.

The themes and arguments of *Perfect: Feeling Judged*

Perfect images and the beauty industry

Perfect: Feeling Judged has argued that ideals of perfection are exerting more pressure than ever before in a world dominated by visual images, entangled with a neoliberal culture preoccupied with individual self-optimization. Young women feel – in their own words – 'overwhelmed' and 'bombarded' by images of perfection, which exert a painful pressure despite these women's awareness, indeed absolute clarity, that the pictures that dominate their feeds are 'not real'. The gap (or, perhaps better, tension or disjuncture) between what young women 'know' and what they 'feel' is one of the recurrent themes *of Perfect: Feeling Judged*, not least because it calls into question one of the dominant policy responses to such anguish, which is to 'teach' greater literacy, criticality and so on. Yet, as I have argued throughout, young people are *already* critical and highly digitally literate. They could teach older adults and policy-makers some things!

Besides the sheer number of images produced and circulating every day, the *proximity* of young women to the images they engage – friends and peers more often than distant, inaccessible 'stars' – amplifies the force of the perfect as a 'horizon of expectation'[3] in a moment in which social comparison is ubiquitous. Moreover, this is reinforced by the everyday *intimacy* of the phone as a medium for such images – always there in your pocket, purse or under your pillow, perpetually serving up new, yet only minutely different, content from the moment you wake up to the moment you finally let the phone slide from your hand as you drift into sleep. The young women I spoke to have been made to believe that a key part of their value lies in their appearance. Their social media practices represent their attempts to succeed in this operating system (let's call it PerfectOS), which is not of their making or choosing, but reflects the values of contemporary neoliberal capitalism steeped in sexism, racism and disablism. To see young women attacked for participating, indicted as 'snowflakes', or allocated the responsibility for change, feels deeply unfair.

Reinforcing the tyranny of the perfect is a beauty industrial complex, almost unrecognizable from a generation ago, in which cosmetic surgeries, injectables, liposuction, lasering, radio-frequency treatments and other procedures have become not just normalized, but *culturally demanded*. I was chastened to learn of the ubiquitous notifications for lip fillers, butt implants, rhinoplasty and cosmetic dentistry being relentlessly pushed to women in their late teens and early twenties 'All. The.Time' as Lynne, 19, vividly put it. As documented in chapter 3, young women are not only subjected by email, targeted ad or push notification to advice that they should work on their appearance via invasive and expensive cosmetic procedures, but they are also 'invited' to submit their selfies to a plethora of apps that will 'rate' them, 'diagnose' their 'problems' and suggest 'personalized' solutions for a multitude of 'defects' picked up by AI and 'machine vision' apps. These apps are themselves predicated on racialized and gendered assumptions, 'baked in' via skin tone biases, preferences for double eyelids, and numerous other disturbing features that pathologize almost everyone.

Seeing and being watched

One of the (many) outcomes of such apps is the emergence of ever more sophisticated visual literacies; what have been referred to as 'forensic' and 'metric' gazes,[4] as well as ever more refined lenses of surveillance. *Perfect: Feeling Judged* has discussed the development of *new ways of seeing* among young women, highlighting the forensic nature of women's practices of looking at themselves and others – the extraordinary level of detail apprehended in just a momentary glance – noting that this mode of seeing subsumes the hostile, evaluative 'judging' gaze that many women themselves feared. These novel visual literacies – particularly of the face – exist in a co-constitutive and mutually reinforcing relation with photo-editing software, the use of which has become a totally routine and taken-for-granted aspect of everyday photographic practice. That is to say that photo-editing apps such as Facetune, which 'improves' and 'enhances' pictures, feeds into the scenario in which an unfiltered or unedited photo can rarely, if ever, feel good enough – even while participants emphasized their commitment to authenticity both as an ethical goal ('it has to look like me', 'I don't want my Insta to be fake') and as a practical consideration ('you don't want to be found out'/have people 'be disappointed in the real you').

As well as seeing in new ways, young women also felt profoundly watched and surveilled both on- and offline. Chapter 4 discussed this in some detail, outlining the felt connections between 'all the eyes and all the hands' (Rosa, 22) in public settings, with the lack of comfort or safety that could involve, and the particular experiences of 'camera culture' in which a night out in a club could feel like being in an episode of a reality TV show because of all the 'camera crews' recording you (Lisa, 20). The watching gaze could be experienced as male, as heterosexual, as white, and also shaped by assumptions about religion. It was experienced also as persistently disablist and as judgemental in relation to body size and shape.

Harassment and hate

The levels of sexual harassment and stalking that young women experienced were closely connected to their sense of being watched. The volume of sexual comments, unsolicited pictures of male genitalia and repeated stalking described by my interviewees were horrifying. Yet they were treated as completely unremarkable. Even so, many young women told me 'I didn't ask for any of this' – the phrase capturing a powerful double meaning – their sense of this as uninvited and unwanted, but also the riposte to a wider sexist culture that persists in telling women they 'asked for it' because of some aspect of their conduct. Alarmingly, digital culture has developed equivalents or corollaries to all the aspects of the blaming of women *offline*. Thus, when women object they are told that their photo was (too) sexy, that they flirted, or what did they expect on a dating app – as if this justified their harassment.

More disturbing still to young women and nonbinary folk was the culture of 'haters' they encountered on social media. Their experiences underscore Sarah Soberaj's argument that hateful harassment is becoming 'normalized',[5] and Brooke Duffy and Emily Hund's analysis of the way that visibility and vulnerability rise in tandem.[6] Not only were my interviewees understandably worried about trolling, but they were also profoundly upset to witness the abuse and hate targeted at *other people*, vividly showing how 'networked misogyny' and racism, disablism and homophobia – the 'toxic technocultures'[7] and 'misogynoir'[8] of social media – has a chilling impact on many people, not just those directly affected – a topic that merits further research. Young women regard the wider treatment of women in the media – legacy media *and* socials – as encoding disciplinary messages about their *own lives* – whether this is Adele, Molly-Mae Hague or Lizzo, as we saw in chapter 4. Tanisha, 26, describes vividly the tormenting effect that accounts 'baiting Black girls' have on her:

> There are so many TikToks baiting Black girls and Black women. It's usually in the form of a trend having guys choose who they would rather date, pitting a Black girl against a non-Black girl. It'll be a split screen giving two categories of women as options and they always toy with us and have one guy hesitating and looking like he is going to go to the Black girl's side, but then no at the last minute he doubles back to the other side. It is really upsetting and disturbing to see. And lots of Black women will comment on those kinds of videos and then some of the creators come back and say oh we didn't mean it like that, but they did, and anyway by then they've got the clicks.

Indeed, experiences of harassment, baiting and hate are unevenly distributed. As in Tanisha's account, they fall with particular force upon women of colour, but also on Muslim women, upon disabled people and on LGBTQ folk who, as the book has shown, are disproportionately subject to harassment and trolling. 'Forces related to gender, race, sexuality, ability and class – tendrils of power – thread through platform communities and cultures, under our skin and through our digital representations', as Warfield et al. elegantly express it.[9]

A particularly distressing aspect of the circulation of attacks in this way is when they are not practised by anonymous others but enacted by friends and peers. Young women told me this is quite different from being 'hated on' because of some aspect of your identity. The experience of being 'talked about' or 'taken down' behind one's back by people you know produced particular anguish among my participants. As I discussed earlier, this might happen via comments or via screenshots that were then shared in a smaller friends' group on WhatsApp or Snapchat. There were many other potential slights and microaggressions – a failure to like content posted, a half-hearted nice comment, or an argument that takes place over a textual medium. Together, these experiences marked friendships as *complicated sites of affection and care, but also competitiveness, judgement and cruelty.* A widespread perception was about how easily friendships can 'go wrong' on digital platforms, where the possibilities for misunderstanding were felt to be ever-present. Two of my interviewees shared stories of losing friendships in this way; others talked about being 'hyper-vigilant' in what they posted in order to avoid this.

The work of being social

This vigilance, of course, takes a lot of work and a great deal of care. Indeed, one of the key themes in *Perfect: Feeling Judged* concerns the sheer amount of labour involved in being on social media. While this has been much-discussed in relation to influencers – particularly YouTubers – it was striking to note similar work being undertaken by a large proportion of the young women I interviewed, even those without very large numbers of followers. They paid constant attention to *planning* posts – their location, the outfit and styling involved, and the timing of the post. They put considerable work into *getting the picture right* – Adija, for example, talked about 30–40 photos being a minimum(!) from which to select the right one. Even night out (group) photos, which had lower 'production values' and were perceived to have less at stake than individual selfies, could routinely take half an hour at the start of an evening out, as Lily and Lisa both regretfully disclosed. *'Post-production'* – involving the selection then editing of photos for posting – could also take significant amounts of time: at the higher end of the spectrum an hour or more *per photo* for Ayeshah and Bipasha. And then there was the labour put into *'engagement'* – checking to see how the post was received, responding to comments, variously deleting or blocking hostile reactions, etc.

I have argued that increasingly many young women on social media have come to resemble micro-celebrities or influencers in their practices and in the various kinds of work they perform to maintain and keep up their digital presence. This includes 'glamour labour', 'visibility labour', 'relational labour', 'authenticity labour' and other forms of 'emotional labour' discussed in chapter 5. Such a shift is also reflected in the language the platforms use, particularly the mainstreaming of the catch-all term 'creators'.[10] We are all creators now, it would seem, blurring the boundaries between those 'aspirational labourers'[11] who seek to make a living from their content, and those who do not (yet) monetize it. This is a significant development.

Feeling judged and anxious

Feeling judged has been a motif throughout the book, and I consider it here along with other emotional experiences. Besides the word 'perfect', the other terms that were recurrent features of the interviews centred on *judgement by others* and *feelings of anxiety*. In addition, I was struck by the frequency and intensity of discussions of depression, of exhaustion and overwhelm, and finally the sense of being both 'trapped' and 'alone'.

The sense of feeling judged by others was almost ubiquitous. As we saw in chapter 6, Bianca, Elizabeth, Eve, Katie, Lily and Lynne spoke eloquently about the fear and the experience of being (negatively) judged by others. India expressed this perhaps most vividly, capturing the intimate relationship between judgement and anxiety, as well as the sense of there being no escape: 'Honestly, it's awful. Every single thing anyone does is judged.' The anxiety that India experienced was discussed by almost all participants as they tried to live up to impossible standards and to post about their lives in the face of pervasive surveillance and judgement. Although several interviewees disclosed mental health challenges in which anxiety was a feature, it seems more productive to think of the ubiquity of feelings of anxiety as part of a social and cultural trend, a contemporary 'structure of feeling',[12] which exceeds or is larger than (while not displacing) individuals' experiences – however distressing these may be. In a much reposted blog titled 'We are all very anxious',[13] the Institute for Precarious Consciousness suggests that each new phase of capitalism has its own 'dominant affect' that is 'a public secret, something that everyone knows, but nobody admits or talks about'. Anxiety currently occupies this role. It is so prevalent among young women that it requires critical and social constructionist understanding, rather than purely a psychiatric response. It should be seen as a 'culture-bound syndrome', maybe even, as Katie Masters puts it, as a 'rational response to the circumstances in which they [young women] find themselves'.[14]

Young women offered vivid and visceral accounts of their experiences of anxiety. They spoke of 'dread' and recounted hearts pounding, adrenaline coursing, whole body blushes and

night-time terrors as they reflected on their everyday experiences on social media. Above all they spoke powerfully of the
huge variety of ways in which they feared 'getting it wrong',
communicating a vivid sense of being just one bad post away
from total humiliation.

Shame, too, was discussed often – both in relation to specific instances of feeling humiliated and, more commonly, in
the widely shared experience of not feeling 'good enough' –
not pretty enough, slim enough, popular enough, successful
enough – with enough money and time to be in nice locations,
in nice clothes, and so on. To hear these extraordinary young
people – interesting, witty and attractive to a person – repeatedly expressing profound feelings of shame and self-contempt
was both upsetting and disturbing. It should not be like this.
To be sure, there were also moments of pride – feelings of
exhilaration that came from a good post, a happy memory, a
photo that you (and others) loved. But these were expressed as
standout moments against a backdrop of worry about living up
to the ideals expected in every aspect of life.

Like the feminist activists interviewed by Hannah
Curran-Troop,[15] Akane Kanai[16] and Christina Scharff,[17] my
participants also described being 'burnt out' and 'exhausted',
despite being on their socials apparently (in most cases) for
fun rather than work or activism. A quotidian experience on
social media was one of 'overwhelm' and 'feeling drained'. Lest
this be seen as a particular outcome of the pandemic, many
explained that Covid had actually 'made things better' in this
respect, facilitating a break and the reduction of pressure. This
finding underscores the extent to which 'we are all influencers
now' – at least in the sense of being pressured to present and
maintain a curated social media presence, and to practise the
plethora of forms of labour required of micro-celebrities. No
wonder, then, so many participants said they felt 'drained'.
In some cases 'drained' could also be a code for depressed
or ashamed, as when Lily described taking one photo after

another of herself in an attempt to get one to post, only to feel that she disliked each one in a new way and thus felt drained and 'spiralled down'.

Struggling alone

A striking feature of many young people's experiences on social media was their experience of loneliness. Like other experiences discussed here, this might seem paradoxical. Several interviewees highlighted *connections with others* and a *sense of community* as central to their social media practices. Alex discussed online LGBTQ+ sites as pivotal to their experience of learning about other nonbinary and trans people's lives. Ches and Ruby also both highlighted their own practices of sharing as being about community and building connections – for Ruby in relation to acrobatic and pole dance communities, for Ches as part of a wide group of friends from school and university. In relation to #BLM activism too, Letitia and Bianca foregrounded their social media activity as a way of being involved in a social movement for change. Yet for the majority of participants – including some of these – their social media were often experienced as sites of difficulty and loneliness rather than support and sociability.

This 'lonely sociality'[18] was sobering to hear about. It relates to the broader sense of being subject to constant judgement, and also to the ambivalent experiences of friendship that young women described. The impression emerging from my interviewees was that there were few places in which, or people with whom, they felt fully safe to be themselves. They expended huge energy in trying to present themselves in the 'right way' on Instagram or Snapchat, but part of the requirement involved effacing the effort involved. When they told me how difficult they found it, I always asked 'do you talk to your friends about this?', and I was dismayed by how often the answer was 'no'. Bianca told me that although she gets advice from a friend and her sister on whether a photo is good enough to post, she doesn't talk with them about how hard she finds things. She said that she found taking part in this research was 'like a detox' because she was able to talk openly about so many difficult issues and experiences. Katie and Lily both said they worried about being honest with their friends about how they feel as it might come across as 'attention seeking'. 'No good will come of that', Katie said; it was better just to pretend to be alright because 'people don't like to admit how hard it is'. Letitia said that she tried to talk with her mum about some of the challenges, but to her mum 'it is unfathomable' why her daughter gets upset about 'something that is not real'. Overlaid on all the other experiences discussed in *Perfect: Feeling Judged*, then, is a sense of *feeling alone* with the difficulties and struggles, a sense of the pressures operating not only to discipline *but also to isolate*. Moreover, even the isolation and loneliness must be disavowed as it is perceived as shameful – and young women described the effort they put into showing that they 'have friends' and 'go out' and are 'not just at home on my own' (Lily).

Critical but caught

Perfect: Feeling Judged on Social Media has highlighted how phenomenally eloquent, knowledgeable and literate young people are about their social media, how erudite and articulate they are in their critiques, yet how caught and trapped they feel. The book started with Elizabeth, in tears and banging her head with her hand as if to try to dislodge the toxic ideas about perfection she felt had taken up residence there, *against her will*. The issue was not a lack of understanding or critique on her part, just as Tanisha's distress about the baiting of Black girls will not be improved by a media literacy programme. How could she be even more literate, more critical of the racist and sexist structures in which she is positioned? What needs to be addressed are the conditions in which young women are operating – these are, I have argued, *conditions of impossibility*.

Young women are *caught* in larger and longer machinations of power that are ever more agile in the forms they take. This book helps to illuminate the broader conjuncture in which my participants are operating – a neoliberal moment, but also one in which there is not only a prohibition against failing, but in which getting something wrong, or even not knowing about something can be constructed as blameworthy. This resonates with other current work which describes this moment as 'perilous' – one in which, as Akane Kanai puts it, 'one is not meant to ask questions if "you don't quite understand something"'.[19] This helps to understand the affective pull of social media with their promise of being 'in the know', rather than left outside. It also helps to illuminate the fear of exposure of various kinds, which led to having to keep up a performance, even in front of intimate friends: the desire to be open, yet the fear of that being used against you, which Zoe Glatt perceptively dubs 'weaponized intimacy'.[20]

Moving on and getting by: beyond perfect

Solutions to the charged and difficult experiences documented in this book are not easy to find. As an academic working in this field, I am frequently asked by journalists and policymakers: what difference would it make to get rid of the 'like' button? Would it help young women if every photo that is digitally altered in some way had to declare this? Is 'body positivity' making a difference? These questions reflect ongoing changes – for example, *in-app* filtering software on TikTok, Instagram and Snapchat does now get labelled with a disclaimer to say which effect has been used; likes are now hidden on Instagram in some regions; and TikTok sends occasional messages to users it thinks are 'too addicted' telling them to

'Go get some extra sleep, turn your phone off, do yourself that favour and have a great night.'[21] Yet such minor interventions might be seen as tokenistic when set against the power of the algorithm that generates content on TikTok's ForYouPage, a model that Instagram is emulating – to the distress of users whose friends' content is now buried in the platform's wider recommendations. When Meta's own research about the links between Instagram use and high levels of emotional distress among a shocking 50 per cent of the platform's 17–21-year-old female users was leaked, its response could hardly be considered robust, as Frances Haugen documented so powerfully in the summer of 2021.[22]

It seems likely that some form of regulation is coming in the UK (and perhaps the EU), at the very least to respond to public outrage about social media platforms 'serving' content about self harm and suicide to young people with depression. To be sure, there are critical questions to be asked about the Online Safety Bill, but can it really be so hard to imagine and create a world in which young people in distress or despair are helped and supported rather than offered content that promotes methods to kill themselves? This seems like a pretty minimal expectation. As for the wider issues – the political, economic, cultural and social changes needed – solutions seem a long way off.

A common response when a problem seems so big and intractable – as with the issues discussed in this book – is to displace it onto those most affected by it so that they are made responsible for the changes and ameliorations necessary, obviating the need to address the cause of the problem itself. For example, people facing injustice or inequality are often enjoined to develop confidence or to practise resilience[23] – instead of to organize to change things. Calling for improved media literacy among young women – who are already so digitally literate[24] – falls into this category and it is emphatically not the solution proposed here. Instead, I will conclude the book by discussing the strategies that young women themselves use to 'get through'. In this last section of the book, I share what they told me about their strategies for coping with social media lives that they sometimes loved but also hated. I also share their suggestions for younger people and their sense of how things are changing.

Body positivity and fighting perfection

One of the key ways that many young people felt they could 'fight back against perfection' (Ruby) was by following 'body positive' influencers. Many participants said that they followed 'curvier and plus size models' and some followed predominantly Black women and LGBTQ+ folk. Signs of progress were seen by some in Rihanna's Fenty brand, in the Crown Act about 'hair discrimination', and other shifts resulting from feminist, antiracist and LGBTQ+ activism. Ruby said she loved body positivity influencer Chessie King, while Alba discussed why she likes Ambar Driscoll, who is described on Influencer Matchmaker as 'passionate about body positivity, often sharing the realities of women's bodies and empowering other women'. Alba said of her:

> She often, she's quite real with her posts, so she'll post a picture of when she first woke up and then when she's eaten, show the difference in bloating and things like that.

Talk about body positivity foregrounded both the importance of widening and diversifying the visibility of particular groups – women of colour, disabled women, fat women, sexual minorities – and, simultaneously the stress on feeling happy, proud and comfortable in one's skin. However, not everyone saw influencers such as King and Driscoll as positive: Ches expressed her anger at the depoliticization of body positivity such that everyone wanted to lay claim to the label even if they looked exactly like the images that activists were trying to challenge – something she saw as represented by King and Driscoll, who are both slim, white, heterosexual and conventionally attractive. A particular bugbear for Ches was the uptake of body positivity assertions by models who were 'stick-thin'. 'How is that supposed to make me feel?' she asked.

Ches's critical perspective was shared by many other participants, who outlined a range of different thoughtful critiques. Bipasha was angry not just at the slowness of change but also at being expected to be pleased by (and grateful towards) the increasing diversity among models. 'Why do we have to think it's amazing just because there's someone with darker skin or a hijab', she said. 'It's not amazing.' She added: 'the blonde size 8 model will get the attention anyway' – highlighting both the small number of models and influencers who break the mould, and also their diminished status in the attention hierarchy. For Sofia and Ayeshah, the issues were around body positivity as 'appropriative' and 'performative', with Ayeshah also highly critical of the hypocrisy of brands who championed diversity yet mistreated and underpaid their workers. Soraya was critical of 'woke-washing' by companies, especially in relation to Black Lives Matter, seeing it as a cynical branding exercise of pretended care. By contrast, Nazanin and Letitia argued that even if that was the case, it did not matter because it is 'so good to see different sizes and ethnicities' (Nazanin).

This brief account indicates the range of perspectives among my participants and their passionate engagement with questions about changing representations.[25] Even though many participants wanted to break free of crushing and punitive norms of feminine appearance, they felt that they could not do so, either because the costs were too high, or because 'the damage has been done' (Elizabeth), or because the forces ranged against them were too powerful, able to appropriate resistance and dissent and sell it back to them as empowerment – as many young women described as a dynamic in relation to Black Lives Matter activism. As Tanisha put it, talking about how the fashion industry had responded to calls for greater diversity, it started off well 'but they've ended up creating another impossible body ideal':

> At first fast fashion companies seemed to be doing something good with their representations as they were challenging the high fashion model stereotype and presenting a really different look. But they've ended up creating yet another impossible body ideal. I don't look like that. It's known as the Instagram baddie look. It crosses racial and ethnic lines but it is a very specific aesthetic usually a curvy woman with pouty lips, a large chest, a small waist, and a big butt. And I worry about the impact it is having on young girls and the pressure it puts on them to go as far as having surgery and other cosmetic procedures such as lip fillers, nose jobs and the BBL [Brazilian Butt Lift].

Quiet refusals

Besides their ambivalent reactions to body positivity trends, there were other ways that young women talked about getting through. This included 'taking a breath', 'going outside', 'keeping a journal', only following 'positive people', making your settings private, not 'feeding the trolls' or responding to negative comments, and – in 20-year-old Soraya's poignant words – 'trying not to care so much'. Young women were far from passive, but were involved in what Lauren Berlant has called 'the defensive, inventive and adaptive activity of getting by' in a world not of their making.[26] The individualism of their coping strategies was striking: in the (devastating) absence of care from any other source, they had become adept at taking care of themselves, through a myriad of micro-strategies and coping skills, built around self-knowledge and hyper-vigilance about their mental health. For many this involved being continuously attentive to their own mental state and then 'taking myself away' (Ella) before the point of complete crisis, whether this is a crisis of overwhelm, of exhaustion, of depression, of anxiety overload. Throughout this book there have been myriad examples of this: Bianca, who deleted posts before going to bed as a way to cope with the anxiety (borne out of her lived experience) about waking up to torrents of abuse; Tanisha, who described how she had become attuned to the exact moment when she should take a break 'otherwise I will get really down'; Nazanin, who counselled 'knowing your own limits and not scrolling, scrolling, scrolling'. There is some-thing phenomenally impressive in these accounts of forms of digital 'self-care', yet also absolutely heartbreaking – for the fact that it is necessary in the first place, for the absence of any other care, and for the loneliness and isolation betokened by these strategies, undertaken alone to pre-empt crisis.

For most it involved a temporary and quiet form of refusal. It could just be turning off notifications or comments, but it also might be taking time out – logging off or quitting, *but not deleting*, the apps. For some it lasted a few hours or a few days, for others it went into two or three weeks, as Lynne described when she was doing her university exams. It was some *time out* – to protect the self and to prioritize other things. But it was difficult and costly to do this. As both Bianca and Lynne described, it could involve hostile questioning and having to refute comments that you had 'had a breakdown'. Yet this simple (if difficult) act of disengagement was young women's *main strategy* for coping with the difficulties of social media lives.

Towards the end of each interview, I asked participants what advice they would give to younger people, or what they might say to their younger selves in light of their own experiences and what they know now. Being able to step away and take time out figured prominently here, but also often mentioned was the idea of having a full life away from social media. Nazanin said: 'you need to be really strong to survive on social media' yet not to get 'your sense of self-worth from how many likes you get' – so having other sources of joy and esteem is vital. For Nazanin it was playing music, for India her pleasure in taking care of animals, for Ruby her love of acrobatics and dance, for Lilian time with her family, and for Holly playing with her two dogs (who also had their own Instagram!). Lisa simply said 'real life is better; it's more forgiving'.

Things are changing: BeReal and TikTok

Besides their strategies of cultivating sources of pleasure and self-worth outside social media, and their attentiveness to moments when it would be best to 'take myself away', there was also a sense that things were constantly changing with new apps, new trends, new forms of resistance. The rise of TikTok, which perfectly coincided with this research, was experienced by some as a kind of antidote to the polished perfection of Instagram. The brevity, accessibility and sheer numbers of videos about absolutely everything meant TikTok was associated with a far greater sense of fun and enjoyment than Instagram, as well as being dubbed 'addictive' by almost everyone. Echoing numerous news and analysis pieces, I was told by two or three interviewees that Instagram is 'dying',[27] and that content creators are moving to TikTok. Participants spoke with something like awe when they reported the amount of engagement they could generate on TikTok almost instantly, while smaller numbers of followers on Instagram took far longer to grow.

BeReal is another app that may have an impact on young women's social media practices. Users are asked to take and post a selfie whenever they receive a timed notification telling them to do so, wherever they are and whatever they are doing. The app had been downloaded 53 million times as I was concluding this book – still small numbers compared with Instagram, Snapchat and TikTok, but it is gradually attracting a younger demographic. I went back to two interviewees – Lynne and Ches – whom I had talked with at the start of this research in June 2020, and I asked them if they used BeReal. They had both recently got it.

Lynne said:

> I use it and so do most of my friends. It's also good because you follow less people on it, so you're more likely to add people you're close with. I think this helps people post more real pictures, as you're not always trying to impress.

Ches said there was still a pressure to post a nice photo, and that often 'people are waiting for a better time of day when they're doing something to actually post' but (unlike on Instagram) 'no one is *overly* precious in how they look'. From her perspective, though, there was a risk of a drift back to the dominance of more perfect pictures. She explained that this came from the realization that the only sanction for posting late was a notification:

> I think the concept at first worked in terms of forcing people to post as and when the timer went off but I think now the sacrifice of posting late – that people get notified about it being late – just isn't really a big deal when you have lots of friends on the app as it happens all the time.

Both Lynne and Ches thought, though, that BeReal was taking some pressure off posting. Ches said that it 'kinda keeps people updated that you're busy and doing something without needing to post something "insta worthy"'. BeReal has instigated a review of the year (like Spotify, Audible and other apps), which shows you a grid of all your posts across the year. This has been 'having a moment' as this book goes to press, and Ches said that lots of her friends posted their BeReal annual catch-up for 2022 on their Instagram – showing the dynamic and complicated nature of social media ecologies, and perhaps also offering hope for a future in which the perfect loses its stranglehold.

Conclusion

Looking to the future I hope there may be a time *without* the dominance of the corporate control of tech companies, without the huge monopolies of Google, Amazon, Meta, Apple and ByteDance. A time when the means of digital production are publicly owned and controlled, run for the benefit of all, without hate, harassment and injustice, and where the digital realm is a 'commons'. However, none of my participants talked of such a radical shift, and their ways of getting by and getting through were far more modest. I hope this book illuminates with empathy and respect how they manage profoundly challenging social media lives, and that it contributes to a wider conversation about building better, more caring and generous futures for all young people.

Notes

Preface

1   The data for this project were collected over a two-year period, with most collected in Spring/Summer 2020. The survey was conducted in May 2020; the first 20 interviews were conducted in May–July 2020; five more interviews were conducted in March–April 2021; and the final interviews were conducted in April–June 2022. In addition, two more participants who did not undertake full interviews gave permission for their words to be used, after talking with me about the project and spontaneously offering accounts of their own experience.

2   By far the most poignant account that I heard came from the father of Molly Russell, a 14-year-old who took her own life after being directed to more and more content about self-harm and suicide by Instagram's algorithm. This has been widely reported in the UK, including in a video made for the BBC: https://www.bbc.co .uk/news/av/uk-46966009. Other powerful accounts that speak to more everyday experiences can be found in former Facebook employee Frances Haugen's 'whistleblowing' in 2021. Speaking to the *Wall Street Journal* for a series titled The Facebook Files, and later giving testimony to the US Congress and the European Parliament, Haugen documented Facebook's knowledge of elec-

tion-related misinformation, vaccine disinformation, the effects of the platforms on young people's mental health, the company's poor record in relation to drug cartels, human trafficking and hate speech, among other things. Of particular relevance to this research is the article by Georgia Wells, Jeff Horwitz and Deepa Seetharaman (2021) 'Facebook knows Instagram is toxic for many teen girls, company documents show', available at: https:// www.wsj.com/articles/facebook-knows-instagram-is-toxic-for -teen-girls-company-documents-show-11631620739?mod=arti cle_inline, accessed 5 December 2022.

3 Dobson, personal communication/unpublished draft 2022.
4 Two useful overviews of research are Keles et al. (2020) and Valkenburg et al. (2022).
5 For example, https://www.theguardian.com/society/2023/jan /01/social-media-triggers-children-to-dislike-their-own-bodies -says-study; https://www.theguardian.com/society/2019/jan/04 /depression-in-girls-linked-to-higher-use-of-social-media
6 Livingstone (2019a).
7 Burgess et al. (2022: 17).
8 Livingstone (2019b: 174).
9 To complicate things further, there is a growing set of highly critical accounts of the role that huge organizations like Google, Amazon, Meta and Apple (GAMA) are playing in developing entirely new forms of capitalism – such as Surveillance Capitalism (Zuboff, 2019), Data Colonialism (Couldry and Mejias, 2019) or Platform Capitalism (Srnicek, 2017). These accounts are important in drawing attention to issues such as the concentration of ownership of information and communication infrastructures in fewer and fewer hands, and the development of unprecedented forms of surveillance and datafication. However, this 'Big Critique' is far removed from the everyday experiences of people using social media, as Burgess et al. (2022) argue persuasively. This book is not focused upon 'The Stack' (the architecture of the internet); on processes of platformization or their economic, technological or legal implications; on state or

corporate surveillance, redefinitions of privacy and the nature of social quantification or algorithmic power. Nor is it focused on the conditions of workers in the internet-fuelled 'gig economy' or the cultural industries more generally. Nor indeed is my concern the nexus or issues related to 'fake news', dis- and misinformation, and 'post-truth'. All these issues are vitally important, to be sure, but they are not my focus here.

10 For example, Wetherell (2012), Thelandersson (2023) Kanai (2018); Pedwell and Whitehead (2012); Kuntsman (2012); Ahmed (2004); and Calder-Dawe et al. (2021).

11 I'm thinking here of bodies of work on digital culture by Moya Bailey, Ruha Benjamin, Julia Coffey, Amy Dobson, Adrienne Evans, Sue Jackson, Akane Kanai, Safiya Noble, Sarah Riley, Jessica Ringrose, Emma Renold, Francesca Sobande, as well as a wealth of scholarship by Crystal Abidin, Jean Burgess, danah boyd, Alice Marwick, Theresa Senft and others. In relation to 'everyday' and 'ordinary' (rather than micro-celebrity) practices, I have been inspired by papers such as Camacho-Miñano et al. (2019); Lavrence and Cambre (2020); Reade (2021); Toffoletti and Thorpe (2021); and Toll and Moss (2021).

12 McRobbie (2015).

13 Halberstam (2011).

Introduction

1 Phrasing and spelling from original.

2 Kanai (2018).

3 This resonates with Haslop et al.'s research (2021), which found very low levels of reporting of harassment. It is also reflected in Ofcom's research.

4 Bordo (1993).

5 Devastating evidence of the crisis increases daily: https:// www.theguardian.com/society/2022/may/22/evidence-of-uks -child-mental-health-crisis-is-stark-and-compelling; https:// www.theguardian.com/uk-news/2023/jan/29/debilitating-effects-pandemic-young-people-uk-health-education-careers; https://

www.bma.org.uk/bma-media-centre/shameful-statistics-show-a-mental-health-crisis-that-is-spiralling-out-of-control-as-demand-far-outweighs-capacity-warns-bma; https://www.the guardian.com/society/2022/jun/28/warnings-of-mental-health -crisis-among-covid-generation-of-students; https://www.hea lth.org.uk/news-and-comment/charts-and-infographics/child ren-and-young-people-s-mental-health. An excellent piece by Sanah Ahsan turns away from individual pathology towards locating mental health as a social issue related to systemic social injustices: https://www.theguardian.com/commentisfree/2022 /sep/06/psychologist-devastating-lies-mental-health-problems -politics

6 Picone et al. (2019).

7 https://ourworldindata.org/explorers/coronavirus-data-ex plorer

8 Office for National Statistics. Prevalence of ongoing symptoms following coronavirus (Covid-19) infection in the UK: 1 June 2022. Available at: www.ons.gov.uk/peoplepopulationandcom munity/healthandsocialcare/conditionsanddiseases/bulletins /prevalenceofongoingsymptomsfollowingcoronaviruscovid19 infectionintheuk/1june2022.

9 https://www.theguardian.com/commentisfree/2022/nov/28/citi zens-advice-cost-of-living-emergency

10 I am grateful to Shani Orgad for drawing my attention to this idea.

11 Paul Frosh and Amit Pinchevski (2014) argue that media witnessing is defined by three overlapping domains of practice: (1) the ways in which ubiquitous audiovisual media make the potential significance of incidentally recorded events available for immediate public reproduction; (2) the organization of interpersonal and mass media as hybrid assemblages of human and technological agents with shifting boundaries that defy traditional models of mass communication, producing ad-hoc communities of attention on a global scale; (3) the incorporation of audiences into a system of perpetual vigilance and

the creation of cosmopolitan risk publics who perceive their commonality through representations of shared vulnerability.

12 Emejulu and Sobande (2019).

13 Sobande (2019).

14 Here, the post #MeToo moment, alongside persistent issues about women's 'believability' are crucial; see Banet-Weiser and Higgins (2023).

15 https://www.openaccessgovernment.org/97-of-women-in-the -uk/105940/

16 The two officers were jailed in December 2021 for two and a half years for what the sentencing judge described as their 'appalling and inexplicable conduct'. Mina Smallman, the sisters' mother, spoke eloquently about how race was a factor in the differential treatment her daughters' murders received compared with that of Sarah Everard: https://www.independent.co.uk/news/uk/ home-news/bibaa-henry-nicole-smallman-sarah-everard-race- police-b1822752.html

17 Sommers (2016); Bailey (2021).

18 Bailey (2021).

19 It is notable how feminists and racial justice activists today work to challenge the invisibilization of Black women through their specific politics around foregrounding the names of victims (and refusing to say the names of perpetrators). When Zara Aleena was murdered in East London in June 2022, the protests were built around the slogan: 'Her Name Was Zara Aleena'. See also #SayHerName.

20 See Yasmin Gunaratnam and Amarjit Chandan's (2016) wonderful celebration of John Berger, *A Jar of Wild Flowers: Essays in Celebration of John Berger*.

21 Haslop et al. (2021) critically discuss the uptake of this pejorative term, and its shift from the Right to the mainstream.

22 I observe these slanging matches with horror, seeing them as clickbait for media, and asking 'who benefits?'.

23 Back (2016).

24 Inspired also by the ethics and integrity of Shani Orgad's (2019) study *Heading Home.*

25 Perhaps the most significant change to the survey that resulted from consulting with two young people of target age about its design was in the introduction of the term 'random browsing' as an activity. This turned out, by some way, to be the activity that young people said they engaged in most of all, and it would have been missed had we stuck with a framing that anticipated more deliberate searching focused on particular categories (e.g. friends, influencers, music, celebrities, etc.).

26 I am grateful to Whitney Francois Cull, who worked with me on designing the survey, for encouraging the use of open questions. I had not anticipated how much time and care participants would devote to sharing their experiences in this way, and am enormously appreciative of this.

27 See, for example, Henwood et al. (1998); Ramazonoglu (2001); Ryan-Flood and Gill (2010); Ryan-Flood et al. (2023).

28 I use the term inclusively, and it is based on self-identification.

29 https://commonslibrary.parliament.uk/2021-census-what-do -we-know-about-the-lgbt-population/; https://www.ethnicity-facts-figures.service.gov.uk/uk-population-by-ethnicity/national -and-regional-populations/population-of-england-and-wales/ latest

30 A note on terminology. The acronym BAME is widely used but highly contested. Other terms in increasing circulation include BIPOC (Black, Indigenous, and people of colour) and global majority. I move between various different terms, with an emphasis upon clarity. Where possible without posing a risk to participants' anonymity, I try to give more specific information about identity and heritage using terms such as British Iranian, white and of Eastern European heritage, and so on. I choose to capitalize the term Black throughout in recognition of its importance as a political identity. More generally, wherever possible I use the terms that participants themselves used as self-descriptions in relation to all aspects of their identity, which

may or may not align with terms in conventional or official discourse.

31 Brah and Phoenix (2004: 76).
32 Hill Collins (1990: 2).
33 Hill Collins and Bilge (2016: 2).

Notes to Chapter 1

1 Ellison and boyd (2013).
2 Baym (2015).
3 boyd and Ellison (2007).
4 Burgess et al. (2018).
5 Sujon (2021: 14) cites Pokemon Go as 'a fascinating example of the convergence between industries (Google and Nintendo), platforms (augmented reality, mobile phones, gaming consoles and apps) and emerging digital socialities'.
6 Statista: https://www.statista.com/statistics/272014/global-soc ial-networks-ranked-by-number-of-users/
7 Senft (2008); Marwick (2016).
8 Banet-Weiser (2018).
9 https://www.theguardian.com/society/2022/may/01/four-in -five-people-in-the-uk-believe-in-being-woke-to-race-and-soc ial-justice
10 https://www.ipsos.com/en-uk/sexual-orientation-and-attitudes -lgbtq-britain (also add what M-J, Laura and I cited; to be added at proof correction stage).
11 Jackson et al. (2020: 1).
12 Van Dijk, 2013, quoted in Leaver et al. (2020).
13 Leaver et al. (2020).
14 See Sujon (2021) for discussion of social media as archives; Prins (2020) on live-archiving the crisis.

Notes to Chapter 2

1 For example, Betterton (1987); Van Zoonen, L. (1994); Gill (2007); Carter et al. (2013); Harvey (2020); and Orbach (2009).
2 Photutorial: https://photutorial.com/statistics/.

3   McRobbie (2015).

4   McRobbie (2009).

5   Widdows (2018).

6   Ahmed (2004).

7   Munt (2007: 2).

8   Ngai (2009).

9   Gill and Cull (2023).

10 Noble (2018); Benjamin (2019).

11 Malik (2001).

12 Noble (2018); hooks (2015); Tate (2005); Jha (2015).

13 Ringrose et al. (2018).

14 Noble (2018).

15 Sastre (2014).

16 Phoenix (2014).

17 Ibid.

18 Thompson (2018).

19 Gaines (2017).

20 See McNicholas Smith (2020).

21 The interview took place before significant new representations of nonbinary characters in *Dr Who* and *Heartstopper*.

22 These issues have been widely reported, with a particular focus on self-harm, suicide and eating disorders. In December 2022, the Center for Countering Digital Hate found that TikTok's algorithms pushed eating disorder and self-harm content to teenagers within three minutes of an interest being shown. https://www.theguardian.com/technology/2022/dec/15/tiktok -self-harm-study-results-every-parents-nightmare

23 Sobande (2023) also notes the money and aesthetic labour that goes into food posting.

24 Scharff (forthcoming); see also Casey and Littler (2022).

25 Banet-Weiser (2018); Banet-Weiser et al. (2019).

26 Rottenberg (2018).

27 Gill (2007, 2016, 2017).

28 Ngai (2009).

Notes to Chapter 3

1 Bordo (1993).
2 Winch (2015).
3 Elias et al. (2017); Banet-Weiser (2018).
4 Gill (2021).
5 Tyler (2011).
6 Nash (2014).
7 'An open letter to the armpit', available at https://www.youtube .com/watch?v=rHgVL3h8BKs.
8 Andrejevic (2015).
9 Gill (2007: 255).
10 It is striking that the gender marketing of vitamin supplements has passed virtually unremarked upon, in comparison to the outrage that has greeted other attempts to offer standardized mass market goods (such as plastic biro pens) to a gendered market: see the outcry and comedic flourishing that greeted A Bic for Her. This is briefly discussed by Benjamin (2019: 20).
11 See Orgad and Gill (2022).
12 Sweeney-Romero (2022); O'Neill (2021).
13 An excellent discussion of fitspo can be found in Evans and Riley (2023); see also Riley et al. (2022).
14 Lupton (2016); Neff and Nafus (2016).
15 Nuffield Council of Bioethics (2017).
16 https://www.harpersbazaar.com/uk/beauty/a39391760/tweak ments-self-esteem/
17 Jones (2012).
18 https://www.theguardian.com/lifeandstyle/2022/sep/28/why -has-britain-fallen-in-love-with-botox-there-is-only-one-way -to-find-out-; https://www.theguardian.com/australia-news/2022 /sep/25/like-a-dystopian-world-inside-the-booming-demand -for-cosmetic-injectables
19 https://www.theguardian.com/australia-news/2022/sep/25/like -a-dystopian-world-inside-the-booming-demand-for-cosmetic -injectables
20 Lee and Clark (2014).

21 https://www.theguardian.com/australia-news/2022/sep/25/like
-a-dystopian-world-inside-the-booming-demand-for-cosmetic
-injectables

22 Maxine Craig (2021) argues that 'orthodontics produce visible inequality'. In her brilliant analysis, she shows how 'the normalization of a form of aesthetic medicine leaves the mark of poverty on the untreated'.

23 TOWIE (The Only Way is Essex) is a British scripted reality TV show, screening since 2010 and known for 'glam, glitz and goss', and for popularizing certain aesthetic trends and beauty treatments.

24 Dosekun (2017: 169–70).

25 Coffey (2021).

26 Toffoletti and Thorpe (2021).

27 Hendry et al. (2022).

28 Wright (2009).

29 Jarrett (2008).

30 Rich and Miah (2014).

31 Camacho-Miñano et al. (2019).

32 Rettberg (2014).

33 Benjamin (2019).

34 Noble (2018).

35 The importing, from evolutionary psychology, of deeply problematic ideas centred on facial symmetry or hip-to-waist ratio as indices of beauty is another example Ana Elias and I discuss elsewhere (Elias and Gill, 2018).

36 Orgad and Gill (2022).

37 https://www.facetouchup.com

38 An example of this kind of app, available on a browser without download, is Plastic Surgery Simulator: https://www.plastic-sur
gery-simulator.com

39 Handyside and Ringrose (2017).

40 Van Dijk, cited in Rettberg (2014).

41 Ajana (2018).

42 Quoted in Kenalemang and Eriksson (2023).

43 Kenalemang and Eriksson (2023).
44 Gill (2021).
45 Lavrence and Cambre (2020).

Notes to Chapter 4
1 Winch (2013).
2 Gill (2019).
3 Flood (2008); O'Neill (2015, 2018); Roberts et al. (2021).
4 Thompson (2018).
5 For a US equivalent, look at social media around 'Are we dating the same guy': https://www.theguardian.com/commentisfree/ 2022/dec/28/women-toxic-online-dates-apps-facebook-groups-dating-platforms
6 https://www.theguardian.com/technology/2023/jan/31/they-fil med-me-without-my-consent-the-ugly-side-of-kindness-videos
7 https://www.gov.uk/government/publications/review-of-sexual -abuse-in-schools-and-colleges/review-of-sexual-abuse-in-scho ols-and-colleges
8 https://yougov.co.uk/topics/politics/explore/issue/Sexual_Assa ult_Sexual_Harrassment
9 Janet Monckton-Smith places stalking at stage 5 of her eight-stage homicide timeline. A 2017 study that looked retrospectively at 358 homicides found that stalking had taken place in 9 out of 10 of the murders. https://www.theguardian.com/society/2022 /mar/30/11-years-10-arrests-at-least-62-women-how-did-brit ains-worst-cyberstalker-evade-justice-for-so-long
10 Thompson (2018).
11 https://www.suzylamplugh.org
12 https://www.nytimes.com/2021/12/30/technology/apple-airtags -tracking-stalking.html
13 'I think I'm being tracked': https://www.tiktok.com/@angel.edge 95/video/7033117374861577477?is_copy_url=1&is_from_web app=v1
14 Ofsted's 2021 rapid review of evidence also found a marked discrepancy between women's and men's perceptions, with

men much less likely to believe that unwanted touching, sexual assault, sexist name-calling and pressure to engage in sexual activities happened to women.

15 Ringrose et al. (2012).
16 Winch (2013, 2015): 'The fragmentation of media audiences into niche markets and evolution of a web 2.0 world where women coproduce and participate in brand spreading, means that the image of the synopticon and panopticon needs development. In digital culture, the panopticon, the synopticon and the paradigms of the many watching the many women, work in harmony. The internalized gaze is honed, perfected and given the opportunity to indulge through synoptic practices such as celebrity scrutiny. This is then devolved among gendered networks through which women can relate and express intimacy. In the gynaeopticon they all turn their eyes on each other in tightly bound networks where they gaze and are gazed upon.'
17 Elias (2016).
18 Quoted in Elias (2016).
19 Elias and Gill (2018).
20 Ringrose and Renold (2010).
21 Elias and Gill (2018).
22 Foucault (1995) wrote: 'It is the fact of being constantly seen, of being able always to be seen, that maintains the disciplined individual in his [sic] subjection.'

Notes to Chapter 5

1 Duffy and Hund (2019); Duffy et al. (2022); Glatt (2021); Bishop (2022); Casey and Littler (2022).
2 Yau and Reich (2018).
3 Leaver et al. (2020).
4 Abidin (2016).
5 Duffy and Hund (2019).
6 Senft (2008); Marwick (2016).
7 Jerslev (2016); see also Reade (2021) and Baker and Rojek (2020).
8 Bucher (2015).

9 Berger (1972); see also Fanon (1952).
10 I am grateful to Rachel O'Neill for talking with me about this.
11 Abidin (2016).
12 Duffy and Sawey (2021).
13 Glatt (2023).
14 There is a parallel here with the status of cosmetic treatments of all kinds. Maxine Craig's (2021) work on orthodontics shows how having work done on your teeth occupies precisely this same space, viz a shift from having to justify cosmetic dentistry to having to account for not having it done, with all the classed and racialized implications.
15 It was striking how often survey responses were written in this impersonal way, almost as though writing about one's own experiences openly would be too painful or humiliating. A similar dynamic is seen in the interviews in which often concerns about the pressures that young people feel would be projected onto a younger age group – whose suffering could then be readily acknowledged and discussed.
16 Baym (2018); Bishop (2022); Duffy and Hund (2019); Elias et al. (2017); Glatt (2021, 2023); Senft and Baym (2015); Wissinger (2015).

Notes to Chapter 6

1 Duffy et al. (2022) argue that women influencers have emerged as 'prominent targets of authenticity policing' and that a recurrent theme of hateblogs is 'fakery', as well as 'thirst traps' (being too sexual to attract attention) and posting too much or too little. It is striking to see the overlaps with my participants' experiences and worries.
2 Banet-Weiser (2012).
3 Orgad and Gill (2022); Thelandersson (2023).
4 I discuss this more fully in Gill (forthcoming b). It resonates with the wider problematic place of 'victimhood' in contemporary UK and US culture – Prins (personal communication) discusses this in relation to celebrity, and see Orgad (2009) for a fasci-

nating discussion of the 'survivor'. Interestingly, there is ever more pushback against the relentless positivity imperatives of Instagram – as discussed by Rebecca Jennings (2023) in *Vox*.

5 Charlie Brooker, 'Nosedive', *Black Mirror*, Season 3, episode 1, aired 2016 https://www.imdb.com/title/tt5497778/; Couldry and Mejias (2019) also discuss the drive towards social quantification, while Fuchs (2014) argues that the like economy creates a like ideology which produces an atmosphere and kind of engagement designed not to be threatening to corporate interests, e.g. advertisers.

6 Bailey (2021); Duffy et al. (2022).

7 Curran-Troop (2023); Glatt (2023).

8 Dabiri (2021).

9 Kanai (2020).

10 Ross (2022). Duffy et al. (2022) also highlight the under-researched nature of troll sites and hate blogs, as well as the prevalence of 'digital horizontal violence'.

Notes to Conclusion

1 I am grateful to Toby Bennett for introducing me to the concept of polycrisis, as briefly discussed by Adam Tooze: https://adam tooze.substack.com/p/chartbook-165-polycrisis-thinking

2 In addition, there were four different Prime Ministers in office between my application for funding and the submission of this manuscript, a period of three years.

3 McRobbie (2015).

4 Elias and Gill (2018); Lavrence and Cambre (2020).

5 Soberaj (2020).

6 Duffy and Hund (2019).

7 Massanari (2017).

8 Bailey (2021).

9 Warfield et al. (2020).

10 Manavis (2022).

11 Duffy (2017); Morgan and Nelligan (2018).

12 Williams (1977).

13 Institute of Precarious Consciousness: https://www.weareplanc
    .org/blog/we-are-all-very-anxious/
14 Masters (2021). This work is part of a long tradition of research
    by feminist scholars that locates psychiatric diagnoses as cultural
    constructions, e.g. Showalter (1985) and Ussher (1991).
15 Curran-Troop (2023).
16 Kanai (2020).
17 Scharff (forthcoming).
18 Hochschild (1983).
19 Kanai (2020).
20 Glatt (2023).
21 Quoted in *The Guardian*: https://www.theguardian.com/techno
    logy/2022/oct/23/tiktok-rise-algorithm-popularity.
22 Vaidhyanathan, S. (2021).
23 Orgad and Gill (2022).
24 Burgess et al. (2022); Dobson (2015).
25 Gill (forthcoming a).
26 Berlant (2013).
27 For example, Lorenz (2019); Huang (2022). My take is that
    accounts of Instagram's death are exaggerated. There are equal
    numbers of commentaries announcing the death of text-based
    social media and the triumph of the visual, epitomized by
    Instagram's cultural logic.

References

Abidin, C. (2016) Visibility labour: Engaging with Influencers' fashion brands and #OOTD advertorial campaigns on Instagram. *Media International Australia*, 161(1), 86–100.

Ahmed, S. (2004) *The Cultural Politics of Emotion*. Edinburgh: Edinburgh University Press.

Ajana, B. (2018) *Self-Tracking: Empirical and Philosophical Investigations*. London: Palgrave.

Andrejevic, M. (2015) Foreword. In R.E. Dubrofsky and S.A. Magnet (eds) *Feminist Surveillance Studies*. Durham, NC: Duke University Press, pp. ix–xviii.

Back, L. (2007) *The Art of Listening*. London: Bloomsbury Press.

Back, L. (2016) *Academic Diary: Or Why Higher Education Still Matters*. Cambridge, MA: MIT Press.

Bailey, M. (2021) *Misogynoir Transformed Black Women's Digital Resistance*. New York: New York University Press.

Baker, S.A. and Rojek, C. (2020) *Lifestyle Gurus: Constructing Authority and Influence Online*. Chichester: John Wiley & Sons.

Banet-Weiser, S. (2012) *Authentic^TM: The Politics of Ambivalence in a Brand Culture*. New York: New York University Press.

Banet-Weiser, S. (2018) *Empowered: Popular Feminism and Popular Misogyny*. Durham, NC: Duke University Press.

Banet-Weiser, S. and Higgins, K. (2023) *Believability: Sexual Violence, Media and the Politics of Doubt*. Cambridge: Polity.

Banet-Weiser, S., Gill, R. and Rottenberg, C. (2019) Postfeminism, popular feminism and neoliberal feminism? Sarah Banet-Weiser, Rosalind Gill and Catherine Rottenberg in conversation. *Feminist Theory*, 21(1), 3–24.

Baym, N. (2015) *Personal Connections in the Digital Age* (2nd edn). Cambridge: Polity.

Baym, N. (2018) *Playing to the Crowd*. New York: New York University Press.

Benjamin, R. (2019) *Race After Technology: Abolitionist Tools for the New Jim Code*. Cambridge: Polity.

Berger, J. (1972) *Ways of Seeing*. London: Penguin.

Berlant, L. (2013) *The Female Complaint: The Unfinished Business of Sentimentality in American Culture*. Durham, NC: Duke University Press.

Betterton, R. (1987) *Looking On: Images of Femininity in the Visual Arts and Media*. London: Pandora Press.

Bishop, S. (2022) Influencer creep. *Real Life Mag*, 9 June. Available at: https://reallifemag.com/influencer-creep/

Bordo, S. (1993) *Unbearable Weight: Feminism, Western Culture, and the Body*. Berkeley, CA: University of California Press.

boyd, d.m. and Ellison, N.B. (2007) Social network sites: definition, history, and scholarship. *Journal of Computer-Mediated Communication*, 13(1), 210–30.

Brah, A. and Phoenix, A. (2004) Ain't I A woman? Revisiting intersectionality. *Journal of International Women's Studies*, 5(3), 75–86.

Bucher, T. (2015) Networking, or what the social means in social media. *Social Media + Society*, 1(1).

Burgess, J., Marwick, A. and Poell, T. (2018) *The SAGE Handbook of Social Media*. London: Sage Publications.

Burgess, J., Albury, K., McCosker, A. and Wilken, R. (2022) *Everyday Data Cultures*. Cambridge: Polity.

Calder-Dawe, O., Witten, K., Carroll, P. and Morris, T. (2021) 'Looks like a lot of awesome things are coming out of the study!':

Reflections on researching, communicating and challenging everyday inequalities. *Methods in Psychology*, 5, 100058.

Camacho-Miñano, M.J., MacIsaac, S. and Rich, E. (2019) Postfeminist biopedagogies of Instagram: Young women learning about bodies, health and fitness. *Sport, Education and Society*, 24(6), 651–64.

Carter, C., Steiner, L. and McLaughlin, L. (eds) (2014) *The Routledge Companion to Media & Gender*. London: Routledge.

Casey, E. and Littler, J. (2022) Mrs Hinch, the rise of the cleanfluencer and the neoliberal refashioning of housework: Scouring away the crisis? *The Sociological Review*, 70(3), 489–505.

Coffey, J. (2021) *Everyday Embodiment: Rethinking Youth Body Image*. Berlin: Springer Nature.

Couldry, N. and Mejias, U.A. (2019) Data colonialism: Rethinking big data's relation to the contemporary subject. *Television & New Media*, 20(4), 336–49.

Craig, M.L. (2021) Orthodontics as expected beauty work. In M.L. Craig (ed.) *The Routledge Companion to Beauty Politics*. London: Routledge, pp. 265–72.

Curran-Troop, H. (2023) 'We live in a capitalist world, we need to survive!': Platform capitalism, feminist cultural entrepreneurs, and pandemic precarity. *Freelance Feminism: Special Issue, European Journal of Cultural Studies*, forthcoming.

Dabiri, E. (2021) *What White People Can Do Next: From Allyship to Coalition*. London: Penguin.

Dobson, A.S. (2015) *Postfeminist Digital Cultures: Femininity, Social Media, and Self-representation*. New York: Palgrave Macmillan.

Dosekun, S. (2017) The risky business of postfeminist beauty. In A.S. Elias, R. Gill and C. Scharff (eds) *Aesthetic Labour*. London: Palgrave Macmillan, pp. 167–81.

Duffy, B.E. (2017) *(Not) Getting Paid to Do What You Love*. New Haven, CT: Yale University Press.

Duffy, B.E. and Hund, E. (2019) Gendered visibility on social media: Navigating Instagram's authenticity bind. In J. Pooley (ed.) *Social Media & the Self: An Open Reader*. Bethlehem, PA: Media Studies Press.

Duffy, B.E. and Sawey, M. (2021) Value, service, and precarity among Instagram content creators. In S. Cunningham and D. Craig (eds) *Creator Culture: An Introduction to Global Social Media*. New York: New York University Press, pp. 135–52.

Duffy, B.E., Miltner, K.M. and Wahlstedt, A. (2022) Policing 'fake' femininity: Authenticity, accountability, and influencer antifandom. *New Media and Society*, 24(7), 1657–76.

Elias, A.S. (2016) *Beautiful Body, Confident Soul: Young Women and the Beauty Labour of Neoliberalism*. Unpublished PhD thesis, submitted to King's College London.

Elias, A.S. and Gill, R. (2018) Beauty surveillance: The digital self-monitoring cultures of neoliberalism. *European Journal of Cultural Studies*, 21(1), 59–77.

Elias, A.S., Gill, R. and Scharff, C. (2017) Aesthetic labour: Beauty politics in neoliberalism. In A. Elias, R. Gill and C. Scharff (eds) *Aesthetic Labour*. London: Palgrave Macmillan, pp. 3–49.

Ellison, N.B. and boyd, d. (2013) 'Sociality through social network sites'. In W.H. Dutton (ed.) *The Oxford Handbook of Internet Studies*. Oxford: Oxford University Press, pp. 151–72.

Emejulu, A. and Sobande, F. (2019) *To Exist is to Resist: Black Feminism in Europe*. London: Pluto Press.

Evans, A. and Riley, S. (2023) *Digital Feeling*. London: Palgrave.

Fanon, F. (1952) *Black Skin, White Masks*. London: Penguin.

Flood, M. (2008) Men, sex, and homosociality: How bonds between men shape their sexual relations with women. *Men and Masculinities*, 10(3), 339–59.

Foucault, M. (1995) *Discipline and Punish: The Birth of the Prison*. New York: Vintage Books.

Frosh, P. and Pinchevski, A. (2014) Media witnessing and the ripeness of time, *Cultural Studies*, 28(4), 594–610.

Fuchs, C. (2014) *Social Media: A Critical Introduction*. London: Sage.

Gaines, A. (2017) *Black for a Day: White Fantasies of Race and Empathy*. Chapel Hill, NC: University of North Carolina Press.

Gill, R. (2007) *Gender and the Media*. Cambridge: Polity.

Gill, R. (2016) Post-postfeminism? New feminist visibilities in post-feminist times. *Feminist Media Studies*, 16(4), 610–30.

Gill, R. (2017) The affective, cultural and psychic life of postfeminism. *European Journal of Cultural Studies*, 20(6), 606–26.

Gill, R. (2019) Surveillance is a feminist issue. In T. Oren and A. Press (eds) *The Routledge Handbook of Contemporary Feminism*. London: Routledge, pp. 148–61.

Gill, R. (2021) Neoliberal beauty. In M.L. Craig (ed.) *The Routledge Companion to Beauty Politics*. London: Routledge, pp. 9–18.

Gill, R. (forthcoming a) 'I try to follow more body positive influencers': Young women talk about body positivity, under submission to *Body Image*.

Gill, R. (forthcoming b) 'I don't want to come across as attention-seeking': Questioning the vulnerability turn on social media. *Journal of Gender Studies*.

Gill, R. and Cull, W. (2023) 'Media do not represent me': Young women's social media lives. In M. Gallagher and A. Vega (eds) *Handbook of Gender, Communication and Women's Human Rights*. Oxford: Wiley Blackwell.

Glatt, Z. (2021) We're all told not to put our eggs in one basket: Uncertainty, precarity and cross-platform labor in the online video influencer industry. *International Journal of Communication*, 16, 1–19.

Glatt, Z. (2023) The intimacy triple bind: Structural inequalities and relational labour in the influencer industry. *Freelance Feminism: Special Issue, European Journal of Cultural Studies*, forthcoming.

Gunaratnam, Y. and Chandan, A. (2016) *A Jar of Wild Flowers: Essays in Celebration of John Berger*. London: Zed Books.

Halberstam, Jack (2011) *The Queer Art of Failure*. Durham, NC: Duke University Press.

Handyside, S. and Ringrose, J. (2017) Snapchat memory and youth digital sexual cultures: Mediated temporality, duration and affect. *Journal of Gender Studies*, 26(3), 347–60.

Harvey, A. (2020) *Feminist Media Studies*. Cambridge: Polity.

Haslop, C., O'Rourke, F. and Southern, R. (2021) #NoSnowflakes: The toleration of harassment and an emergent gender-related digital divide in a student online culture. *Convergence*, 27(5), 1418–38.

Hendry, N.A., Hartung, C. and Welch, R. (2022) Health education, social media, and tensions of authenticity in the 'influencer pedagogy' of health influencer Ashy Bines. *Learning, Media and Technology*, 47(4), 427–39.

Henwood, K., Griffin, C. and Phoenix, A (eds) (1998) *Standpoints and Differences: Essays in the Practice of Feminist Psychology*. London: Sage Publications.

Hill Collins, P. (1990) *Black Feminist Thought*. New York: Routledge.

Hill Collins, P. and Bilge, S. (2016) *Intersectionality*. Cambridge: Polity.

Hochschild, A. (1983) *The Managed Heart: Commercialization of Human Feeling*. Berkeley, CA: University of California Press.

hooks, b. (2015) Selling hot pussy: Representations of black female sexuality in the cultural marketplace. In *black looks: race and representation*. New York: Routledge, pp. 122–32.

Huang, K. (2022) The rise of the 0.5 selfie. *New York Times*, 6 March. Available at: https://www.nytimes.com/2022/06/23/technology/0-5-selfie.html

Jackson, S., Bailey, M. and Foucault Welles, B. (2020) *#HashtagActivism: Networks of Race and Gender Justice*. Cambridge, MA: MIT Press.

Jarrett, K. (2008) Beyond Broadcast Yourself™: The future of Youtube, *Media International Australia*, 126(1), 132–44.

Jennings, R. (2023) 'Hater' doesn't have to be a dirty word. Available at: https://www.vox.com/the-goods/23559396/talia-lichtstein-spreading-negativity-haters.

Jerslev, A. (2016) Media Times| In the time of the microcelebrity: Celebrification and the YouTuber Zoella. *International Journal of Communication*, 10, 5233–51.

Jha, M. (2015) *The Global Beauty Industry: Colorism, Racism, and the National Body*. Abingdon, Oxon: Routledge.

Jones, M. (2012) Cosmetic surgery and the fashionable face. *Fashion Theory*, 16(2), 193–209.

Kanai, A. (2018) *Gender and Relatability in Digital Culture: Managing Affect, Intimacy and Value.* New York: Springer.

Kanai, A. (2020) Between the perfect and the problematic: Everyday femininities, popular feminism, and the negotiation of intersectionality. *Cultural Studies*, 34(1), 25–48.

Keles, B., McCrae, N. and Grealish, A. (2020) A systematic review: The influence of social media on depression, anxiety and psychological distress in adolescents. *International Journal of Adolescence and Youth*, 25(1), 79–93.

Kenalemang-Palm, L. and Eriksson, G. (2023) How cosmetic apps fragmentize and metricize the female face: A multimodal critical discourse analysis. *Discourse and Communication*, forthcoming.

Kuntsman, A. (2012) Introduction: Affective fabrics of digital cultures. In A. Karatzogianni and A. Kuntsman (eds) *Digital Cultures and the Politics of Emotion: Feelings, Affect and Technological Change.* Basingstoke: Palgrave Macmillan, 1–17.

Lavrence, C. and Cambre, C. (2020) 'Do I look like my selfie?': Filters and the digital-forensic gaze. *Social Media + Society*, 6(4).

Leaver, T., Highfield, T. and Abidin, C. (2020) *Instagram: Visual Social Media Cultures.* Cambridge: Polity.

Lee, S.Y. and Clark, N. (2014) The normalization of cosmetic surgery in women's magazines from 1960 to 1989. *Journal of Magazine Media*, 15(1).

Livingstone, S. (2019a) *Are the kids alright? Intermedia*, 47(3), 10–14.

Livingstone, S. (2019b) Audiences in an age of datafication: Critical questions for media research. *Television and New Media*, 20(2), 170–83.

Lorenz, T. (2019) The Instagram aesthetic is over. *The Atlantic*, 23 April. https://www.theatlantic.com/technology/archive/2019/04/influencers-are-abandoning-instagram-look/587803/

Lupton, D. (2016) *The Quantified Self.* Cambridge: Polity.

Mac, R. and Hill, K. (2021) Are Apple AirTags being used to track people and steal cars. *New York Times*, 30 December. Available at: https://www.nytimes.com/2021/12/30/technology/apple-airtags-tracking-stalking.html

Malik, S. (2001) *Representing Black Britain: Black and Asian Images on Television*. London: Sage.

Manavis, S. (2022) The decline of text-based social media. *New Statesman*, 9 November. Available at: https://www.newstatesman.com/social-media/2022/11/decline-social-media-text-post

Marwick, A.E. (2016) You may know me from YouTube: (Micro-) celebrity in social media. In P.D. Marshall and S. Redmond (eds) *A Companion to Celebrity*. Chichester: John Wiley & Sons, pp. 333–50.

Massanari, A. (2017) #Gamergate and The Fappening: How Reddit's algorithm, governance, and culture support toxic technocultures. *New Media & Society*, 19(3), 329–46.

Masters, K. (2021) *Putting the Social in Social Anxiety Disorder: Exploring Women's Experiences from a Feminist and Anti-Psychiatry Perspective*. Unpublished PhD thesis, University of Birmingham.

McNicholas Smith, K. (2020) *Lesbians on Television: New Queer Visibility & the Lesbian Normal*. Bristol: Intellect Books.

McRobbie, A. (2009) *The Aftermath of Feminism: Gender, Culture and Social Change*. London: Sage.

McRobbie, A. (2015) Notes on the perfect: Competitive femininity in neoliberal times. *Australian Feminist Studies*, 30(83), 3–20.

Morgan, G. and Nelligan, P. (2018) *The Creativity Hoax: Precarious Work in the Gig Economy*. London: Anthem Press.

Munt, S. (2007) *Queer Attachments: The Cultural Politics of Shame*. Abingdon, Oxon: Routledge.

Nash, M. (2014) Picturing mothers: A photovoice study of body image in pregnancy. *Health Sociology Review*, 23(3), 242–53.

Neff, G. and Nafus, D. (2016) *Self-tracking*. Cambridge, MA: MIT Press.

Ngai, S. (2009) *Ugly Feelings*. Cambridge, MA: Harvard University Press.

Noble, S. (2018) *Algorithms of Oppression*. New York: New York University Press.

Nuffield Council on Bioethics (2017) Cosmetic Procedures: Ethical

Issues. Available at: https://www.nuffieldbioethics.org/publi
cations/cosmetic-procedures

O'Neill, R. (2015) Whither critical masculinity studies? Notes on inclusive masculinity theory, postfeminism, and sexual politics. *Men and Masculinities*, 18(1), 100–20.

O'Neill, R. (2018) *Seduction: Men, Masculinity and Mediated Intimacy*. Cambridge: Polity.

O'Neill, R. (2021) 'Glow from the inside out': Deliciously Ella and the politics of 'healthy eating'. *European Journal of Cultural Studies*, 24(6), 1282–303.

Orbach, S. (2009) *Bodies*. London: Picador.

Orgad, S. (2009) The survivor in contemporary culture and public discourse: A genealogy. *The Communication Review*, 12(2), 132–61.

Orgad, S. (2019) Heading Home: Motherhood, Work and the Failed Promise of Equality. New York: Columbia University Press.

Orgad, S. and Gill, R. (2022) *Confidence Culture*. Durham, NC: Duke University Press.

Pedwell, C. and Whitehead, A. (2012) Affecting feminism: Questions of feeling in feminist theory. *Feminist Theory*, 13(2), 115–29.

Phoenix, A. (2014) Colourism and the politics of beauty. *Feminist Review*, 108, 97–105.

Picone, I., Kleut, J., Pavlíčková, T., Romic, B., Møller Hartley, J. and De Ridder, S. (2019) Small acts of engagement: Reconnecting productive audience practices with everyday agency. *New Media & Society*, 21(9), 2010–28.

Prins, A. (2020) Live-archiving the crisis: Instagram, cultural studies and times of collapse. *European Journal of Cultural Studies*, 23(6), 1046–53.

Ramazonoglu, C. (2001) *Feminist Methodology: Challenges and Choices*. London: Sage Publications.

Reade, J. (2021) Keeping it raw on the 'gram: Authenticity, relatability and digital intimacy in fitness cultures on Instagram. *New Media & Society*, 23(3), 535–53.

Rettberg, J. (2014) *Seeing Ourselves Through Technology: How We Use*

Selfies, Blogs and Wearable Devices to See and Shape Ourselves. London: Palgrave.

Rich, E. and Miah, A. (2014) Understanding digital health as public pedagogy: A critical framework. *Societies,* 4(2), 296–315.

Riley, S., Evans, A. and Robson, M. (2022) *Postfeminism and Body Image.* London: Routledge.

Ringrose, J. and Renold, E. (2010) Normative cruelties and gender deviants: The performative effects of bully discourses for girls and boys in school. *British Educational Research Journal,* 36(4), 573–96.

Ringrose, J., Gill, R., Livingstone, S. and Harvey, L. (2012) A qualitative study of children, young people and 'sexting': a report prepared for the NSPCC. London: National Society for the Prevention of Cruelty to Children.

Ringrose, J., Tolman, D. and Ragonese, M. (2019) Hot right now: Diverse girls navigating technologies of racialized sexy femininity. *Feminism & Psychology,* 29(1), 76–95.

Roberts, S., Ravn, S., Maloney, M. and Ralph, B. (2021) Navigating the tensions of normative masculinity: Homosocial dynamics in Australian young men's discussions of sexting practices. *Cultural Sociology,* 15(1), 22–43.

Ross, L. (2022) *Calling in the Calling Out Culture: Detoxing Our Movement.* New York: Simon & Schuster.

Rottenberg, C. (2018) *The Rise of Neoliberal Feminism.* Oxford: Oxford University Press.

Ryan-Flood, R. and Gill, R. (2010) *Secrecy and Silence in the Research Process: Feminist Reflections.* London: Routledge.

Ryan-Flood, R., Crowhurst, I. and James-Hawkins, L. (eds) (2023) *Difficult Conversations: A Feminist Dialogue.* London: Routledge.

Sastre, A. (2014) Towards a radical body positive. *Feminist Media Studies,* 14(6), 929–43.

Scharff, C. (forthcoming) Creating content for Instagram: Digital feminist activism and the politics of class.

Senft, T.M. (2008) *Camgirls: Celebrity and Community in the Age of Social Networks.* New York: Peter Lang.

Senft, T.M. and Baym, N.K. (2015) What does the selfie say? Investigating a global phenomenon. *International Journal of Communication*, 9, 1588–606.

Showalter, E. (1985) *The Female Malady*. London: Virago.

Sobande, F. (2019) Woke-washing: 'Intersectional' femvertising and branding 'woke' bravery. *European Journal of Marketing*, 54(11), 2723–45.

Sobande, F. (2023) *Consuming Crisis: Commodifying Care and Covid-19*. London: Sage.

Soberaj, S. (2020) *Credible Threat: Attacks against Women Online and the Future of Democracy*. Oxford: Oxford University Press.

Sommers, Z. (2016) Missing white woman syndrome: An empirical analysis of race and gender disparities in online news coverage of missing persons. *Journal of Criminal Law and Criminology*, 105(2), 275–314.

Srnicek, N. (2017) *Platform Capitalism*. Cambridge: Polity.

Sujon, Z. (2021) *The Social Media Age*. Thousand Oaks, CA: Sage Publishing.

Sweeney-Romero, K.M. (2022) Wellness TikTok: Morning routines, eating well, and getting ready to be 'that girl'. In T. Boffone (ed.) *TikTok Cultures in the United States*. London: Routledge, pp. 108–16.

Tate, S. (2005) *Black Skins, Black Masks Hybridity, Dialogism, Performativity*. Abingdon, Oxon: Routledge.

Thelandersson, F. (2023) *21st Century Media and Female Mental Health: Profitable Vulnerability and Sad Girl Culture*. New York: Springer.

Thompson, L. (2018) 'I can be your Tinder nightmare': Harassment and misogyny in the online sexual marketplace. *Feminism & Psychology*, 28(1), 69–89.

Toffoletti, K. and Thorpe, H. (2021) Bodies, gender, and digital affect in fitspiration media. *Feminist Media Studies*, 21(5), 822–39.

Toll, M. and Moss, N. (2021) More than meets the eye: A relational analysis of young women's body capital and embodied understandings of health and fitness on Instagram. *Qualitative Research in Sport, Exercise and Health*, 13(1), 59–76.

Tyler, I. (2011) Pregnant beauty: Maternal femininities under neoliberalism. In R. Gill and C. Scharff (eds) *New Femininities: Postfeminism, Neoliberalism and Subjectivity*. Basingstoke: Palgrave Macmillan, pp. 21–36.

Ussher, J. (1991) *Women's Madness: Misogyny or Mental Illness*. Harmondsworth: Penguin.

Vaidhyanathan, S. (2021) Leaks exposed how toxic Facebook and Instagram are to teen girls and, well, everyone. *The Guardian*, 18 September. Available at: https://www.theguardian.com/com mentisfree/2021/sep/18/facebook-instagram-zuckerberg-teena gers

Valkenburg, P., Meier, A. and Beyens, I. (2022) Social media use and its impact on adolescent mental health: An umbrella review of the evidence. *Current Opinions in Psychology*, 44, 58–68.

Van Zoonen, L. (1994) *Feminist Media Studies*. Thousand Oaks, CA: Sage.

Warfield, K., Abidin, C. and Cambre, C. (2020) *Mediated Interfaces: The Body on Social Media*. London: Bloomsbury.

Wetherell, M. (2012) *Affect and Emotion: A New Social Science Understanding*. London: Sage Publications.

Widdows, H. (2018) *Perfect Me: Beauty as an Ethical Ideal*. Princeton, NJ: Princeton University Press.

Williams, R. (1977) Structures of feeling. In *Marxism and Literature*. Oxford: Oxford University Press.

Winch, A. (2013) *Girlfriends and Postfeminist Sisterhood*. Basingstoke: Palgrave Macmillan.

Winch, A. (2015) Brand intimacy, female friendship and digital surveillance networks. *New Formations*, 84, 228–45.

Wissinger, E. (2015) *This Year's Model: Fashion, Media, and the Making of Glamour*. New York: New York University Press.

Wright, J. (2009) Biopower, biopedagogies and the obesity epidemic. In J. Wright and V. Harwood (eds) *Biopolitics and the 'Obesity Epidemic': Governing Bodies*. New York: Routledge, pp. 1–14.

Yau, J.C. and Reich, S.M. (2018) Are the qualities of adolescents' offline friendships present in digital interactions? *Adolescent Research Review*, 3, 339–55.

Zuboff, S. (2019) *The Age of Surveillance Capitalism: The Fight for a Human Future at the New Frontier of Power*. London: Profile Books.